Contents

1	Using GIS	4
1.1	John Snow, doctor and detective	5
1.2	Meet GIS	6
1.3	GIS in fighting crime	7
1.4	More about the data	8
1.5	Other uses for GIS	9

2	Population	10
2.1	Our numbers are growing fast	11
2.2	So where is everyone?	12
2.3	The population of the UK	13
2.4	Population around the world	14
2.5	Our impact on our planet	15
2.6	What does the future hold?	16

3	Urbanisation	17
3.1	How our towns and cities grew	18
3.2	Manchester's story – part 1	19
3.3	Manchester's story – part 2	20
3.4	Urbanisation around the world	21
3.5	Why do people move to urban areas?	22
3.6	It's not all sunshine!	23
3.7	Life in the slums	24
3.8	A city of the future?	25

4	Coasts	26
4.1	Waves and tides	27
4.2	The waves at work	28
4.3	Landforms created by the waves	29
4.4	The coast and us	30
4.5	Your holiday in Newquay	31
4.6	Under threat from the sea	32
4.7	How long can Happisburgh hang on?	33
4.8	Protecting places from the sea	34

5	Weather and climate	35
5.1	It's the weather!	36
5.2	So what causes weather?	37
5.3	Measuring the weather	38
5.4	More about rain… and clouds	39
5.5	Air pressure	40
5.6	Why is our weather so cha	
5.7	A winter of storms	
5.8	From weather to climate	
5.9	The factors that influence climate	44
5.10	Climates around the world	45

6	Our warming planet	46
6.1	Earth's temperature through the ages	47
6.2	Global warming	48
6.3	Climate change	49
6.4	It's happening already!	50
6.5	Who will suffer most?	51
6.6	So what can we do?	52

7	Asia	53
7.1	What and where is Asia?	54
7.2	Asia's countries and regions	55
7.3	A little history	56
7.4	What's Asia like?	57
7.5	Asia's physical features	58
7.6	Asia's population	59
7.7	Asia's biomes	60

8	Southwest China	61
8.1	China: an overview	62
8.2	The rise of China	63
8.3	China's Southwest region	64
8.4	Chongqing	65
8.5	Life in Chongqing	66
8.6	Tops for biodiversity!	67
8.7	Tibet	68
8.8	All change in Tibet	69
8.9	The rivers and dams	70

3

1 Using GIS

pages 4-5

You probably thought that a map was something that showed where places and other features in the world are found. With a GIS, however, maps can do so much more. There are three main types of map

- **Location maps** answer the question 'Where am I?'
- **Navigation maps** answer the question 'How do I get there'?
- **Spatial relationship (GIS) maps** are digital and help to answer the question – 'How are these things related or connected'?

1 For each of the following circle which of the above you would need to use.

This is my route to school (location /(navigation)/ GIS)

I want to drive to Cornwall on holiday (location /(navigation)/ GIS)

Where is Leeds? ((location)/ navigation / GIS)

Can I grow crops here? (location / navigation /(GIS))

This is where I live ((location)/ navigation / GIS)

Where is the best place for our new recycling plant? (location / navigation /(GIS))

Choose one of your answers and explain why you chose the answer you did.

Pupils should justify one of the answers given above.

2 GIS stands for Geographic Information System and there is a worldwide GIS Day that takes place in November each year. In the box below design an attractive postcard that would help advertise the day.

Design should be interesting to look at, feature aspects of GIS and should inform and attract the reader to the event.

4

1.1 John Snow, doctor and detective

This is about Doctor Snow's very clever use of maps over 160 years ago.

pages 6-7

1 Look at these statements. They describe what Doctor Snow did but are jumbled up. Write a number from 1-7 in the box to put them in the correct order.

Work began on the sewage system in 1859 **7**

Using a map of the area, Doctor Snow marked all the households where people had died **3**

On 31 August 1854, a cholera outbreak hit the area called Soho, in London **1**

Doctor Snow looked for patterns **5**

He also marked where the water pumps were. **4**

Within ten days, 500 were dead **2**

Doctor Snow thought that the water from the Broad Street pump was infected **6**

2 Imagine it is 1857 and you are Doctor Snow. Write a letter to the government explaining why a new sewage system should be built. Try to be as persuasive as you can, and use facts and figures to support your ideas.

The letter should draw on evidence shown above to try to persuade the government to build a sewage system, alerting them to the benefits that such a project should bring. The best answers will use persuasive language and use facts and figures to reinforce the argument put forward.

Using GIS

1.2 Meet GIS

This is about the exciting use of maps on a computer.

pages 8-9

Imagine you are part of a group who are planning what should happen if a flood occurs in your town. You are working with a GIS expert to help develop your 'local' GIS map. The GIS expert suggests that you can choose six of the following layers on your GIS map:

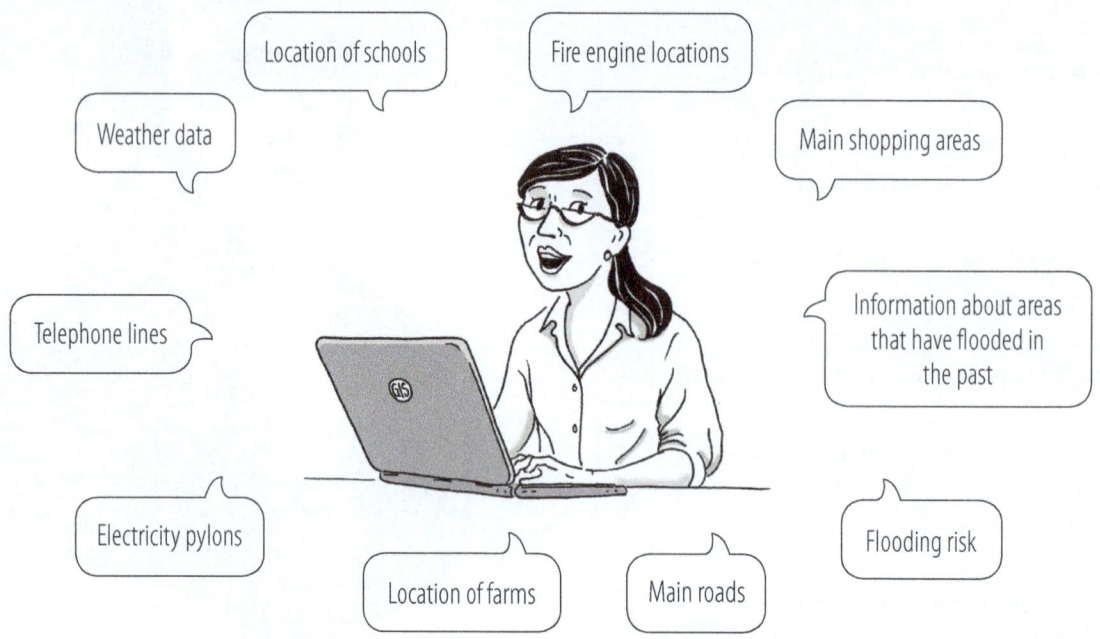

1. Colour in the six bubbles to show the layers of information that you would want on your GIS map. *Six layers should be chosen and coloured in.*

2. Decide which you think is the most important information. Give reasons to explain your choice.

   I think the most important information is _____

   One layer should be chosen with its importance underlined and more than one reason given in explanation.

3. Choose one of the layers that you decided was not needed on your map. Give reasons for your choice.

   I did not include _____ because _____

   One layer should be identified with more than one reason for its non-inclusion given.

4. Can you think of one other piece of information that would be helpful to add as a layer to your GIS? In the space below state your layer and say why it would be useful.

   Students should identify another layer that they would feel is of benefit, and gives a reason(s) behind their choice. A range of answers are possible, such as location of rivers or contour maps.

6 Using GIS

.3 GIS in fighting crime

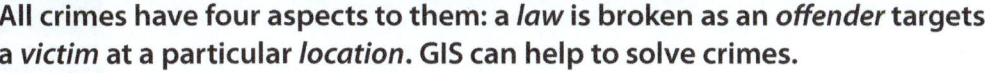

pages 10-11

All crimes have four aspects to them: a *law* is broken as an *offender* targets a *victim* at a particular *location*. GIS can help to solve crimes.

1 Write your own definition of an offender and a victim in the spaces below.

An offender is ... *a person that does something wrong and against the law and who causes problems for others.*

A victim is ... *a person harmed, injured, or killed as a result of a crime.*

2 The map in the student book shows where crimes were committed. Look at the crimes recorded in grid square 1137. Write in the blog post below giving advice to people visiting the area. The blog post has been started for you.

> **Tip:** Be specific. Look at the types of crime and think about how people could avoid becoming crime victims.

| Home | Blog Archive | About | 🔍 |

Keeping safe

When visiting this area it is really important that you keep safe by...

Advice should relate to the crimes identified within the grid square which are predominately vandalism, assault and break-ins.

3 You are in charge of controlling crime in the area. Where would you put most of your police resources? Name specific locations from the map and give reasons for your answer.

Pupils should identify grid squares to prioritise for policing based upon the map evidence. These may be 1137 (Central Square), 1436 (playing fields) or the squares along the High Street. Pupils should give specific reasons for each of the locations they give, explaining why police resources would help to alleviate crime.

Using GIS **7**

1.4 More about the data

The world is increasingly data rich. GIS helps us to effectively use data to solve problems.

pages 12–13

1 GIS needs data. Fill in the gaps in the following passage using words from the box beneath. Use the student book to help you.

The main purpose of GIS is to display __data__ on a map, helping us to find __patterns__, make __decisions__ and decide on __actions__ to take. GIS data is very well-organised in __layers__. Each layer has one __theme__. A GIS allows us to turn layers on and off, so that we are only seeing the layers that are __helpful__ to us.

theme decisions maps helpful actions layers data patterns

2 Look at these data layers for a new GIS investigation. People were asked in a survey if they would like to see a new shopping centre built.

Describe one investigation that this information would allow you to do. Explain how each of the data layers would help you.

- survey results
- average income
- where shoppers live
- main roads
- bus routes
- age of residents
- trees/woodland
- Ordnance Survey map data

Answers should suggest an investigation, and then explain how each of the eight layers would help to make the final decision. A typical answer might be:

A possible investigation might be to see where the best place for a new shopping centre might be, and the OS map data would be central in helping to make this decision. Survey results would show people's opinions about location and type, and average income would help show how much money people may have to spend in the new development. Access to the shopping centre is important, so a knowledge of where people live and access routes are both important pieces of information. Facilities for different groups of people will need to be catered for, but the development needs to be balanced with its impact on the environment.

Using GIS

.5 Other uses for GIS

The use of GIS affects our lives in many ways that we perhaps do not know!

1 Imagine you are a parcel! You are being sent on a journey from the Netherlands to Sheffield, in Yorkshire. Your route is shown below.

Scheduled Delivery: Tuesday, 10/12/2013, By End of Day
Last Location: Sheffield, United Kingdom, Tuesday, 10/12/2013

▼ Additional Information

Shipped/Billed On:	06/12/2013
Type:	Package
Weight:	2.30 kgs

▼ Shipment Progress

Location	Date	Local Time	Activity
Sheffield, United Kingdom	10/12/2013	6:07	Out for Delivery
	10/12/2013	4:45	Arrival scan
Tamworth, United Kingdom	10/12/2013	3:21	Departure Scan
Tamworth, United Kingdom	09/12/2013	20:32	Arrival Scan
Barking, United Kingdom	09/12/2013	17:18	Departure Scan
	09/12/2013	12:33	Arrival Scan
Brussels, Belgium	09/12/2013	8:33	Departure Scan
Brussels, Belgium	07/12/2013	3:21	Arrival Scan
Eindhoven, Netherlands	06/12/2013	23:45	Departure Scan
	06/12/2013	20:26	Origin Scan
Netherlands	06/12/2013	14:07	Order Processed: Ready for UPS

7. Travel by van to customer
6. Travel by lorry to Sheffield airport
5. Travel by air to East Midland airport, then by van to Tamworth.
4. Travel by lorry to Barking, London
3. Travel by air to Heathrow airport, London
2. Travel by lorry to Brussels.
1. Travel by van to Eindhoven

In the space below, write a description of how GIS helped your journey.

Pupils should describe the role of GIS in the parcel's journey. Typical answers are likely to include the role of GIS in satellite navigation systems for the modes of transport in each of the stages. The importance of GIS in helping to move transport through the use of sensors on roads and railways, bridges and tunnels and at airports may also be mentioned. Finally, pupils may start to explain the value of GIS in speeding up deliveries, so ensuring that valuable time is utilised effectively.

Tip: Think about when your bar code would be scanned and who would be given that information – driver, parcel depot, customers.

Using GIS 9

2 Population

pages 16-17

1 Are these statements true or false? Put a tick in the correct box.

		True	False
a	We are not living as long as we used to do	☐	☑
b	Our numbers have been growing fast for 250 years	☑	☐
c	The population is falling in some countries	☑	☐
d	The world's population is unevenly spread	☑	☐
e	Our growing population has an impact upon the earth	☑	☐
f	The world's population is expected to reach 6 billion by 2025	☐	☑
g	5 000 new babies are born every single day	☐	☑

2 Distribution means the way in which something is shared out among a group or spread over an area. Write you own definition of population distribution in the space below. Compare your answer with a partner. Which of you has the most accurate definition?

Two possible definitions are:
a) the arrangement or spread of people living in a given area
b) how the population of an area is arranged according to
    variables such as age, race, or sex.

3 Imagine the earth could write a letter to us. What do you think it would say about how it is expected to cope with the growing population?

Most students will be aware of the impact that we have had on the environment. Some may make the argument on behalf of the Earth for more sustainable development.

2.1 Our numbers are growing fast

This is about population change.

1. Use arrows to link the key terms below to their correct definitions.

   birth rate → the number of births each year for every 1000 people

   natural increase → birth rate minus death rate

   death rate → the number of deaths each year for every 1000 people

2. Draw a coffin shape next to those factors below which you think would increase the death rate. Draw a baby shape next to those factors which would increase the birth rate. Two have been done for you.

   - dirty water
   - young age of marriage
   - reliable food supply
   - lots of disease
   - children begin working when young
   - war
   - no contraception
   - not enough food

3. Write down two factors that you think would reduce the death rate. Explain why.

Factor	Explanation
Better medical care	People will live longer. They will still die! But their deaths will be spread over many years.
Better access to clean water	Water-borne diseases are a major cause of childhood mortality.

4. Using the table below, calculate which countries have a rising population, and which a falling one. Take away the death rate from the birth rate. One has been done for you.

	Birth rate/1000	Death rate/1000	Natural increase/1000
Ghana	42	33	9
Italy	7	9	−2
UK	9	10	−1
Mexico	21	11	10
India	30	18	12

Population 11

2.2 So where is everyone?

This is about countries with lots of people, and places with hardly any.

1. We call countries with lots of people densely populated, and countries with few people s p a r s e l y populated.

2. Look at the map. You will notice that Greenland and India have been left blank. Use the key to shade in the country that you think is densely populated, and leave the other country blank. *India is the more densely populated.*

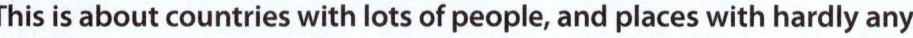

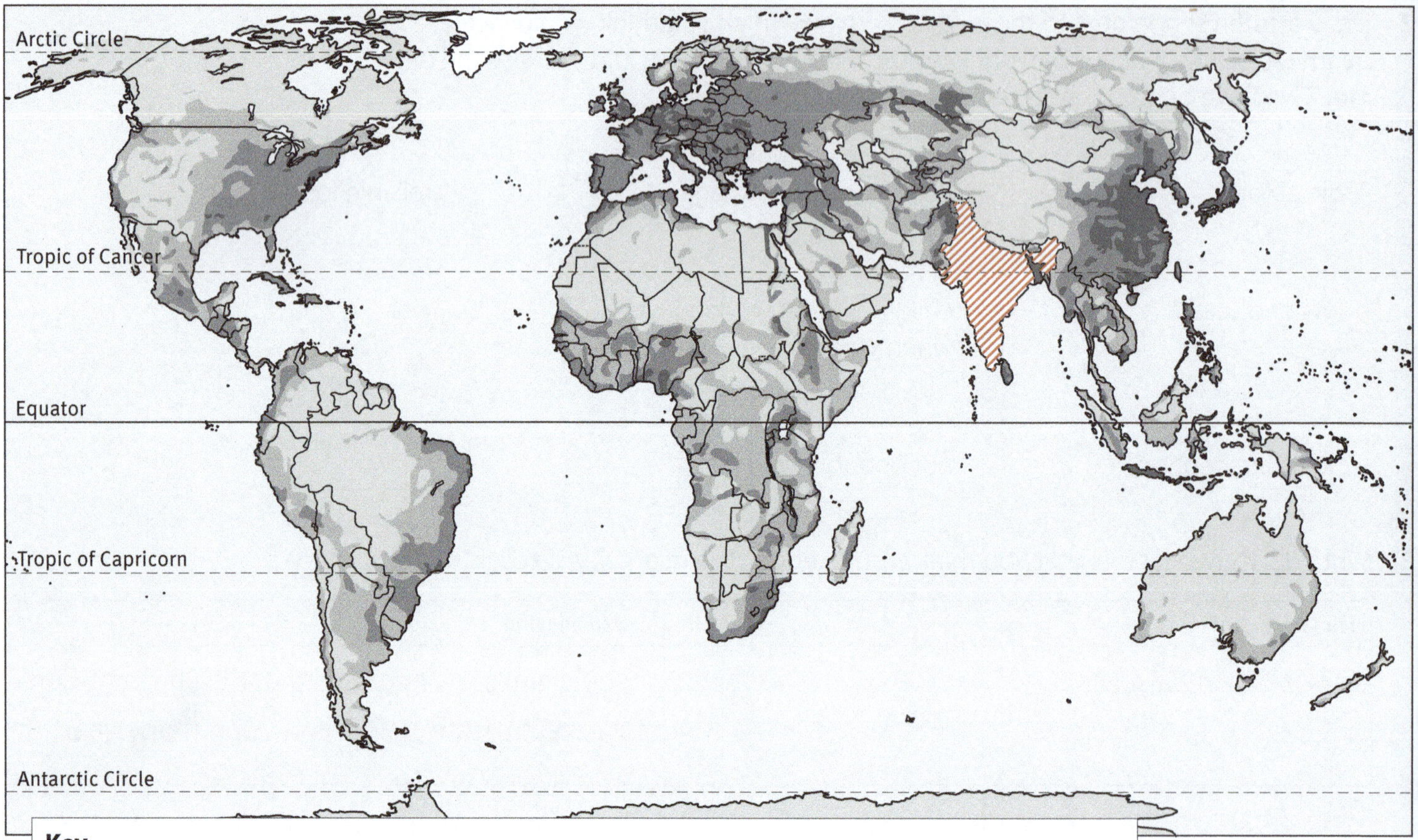

Key
- very densely populated areas with large cities and towns
- fairly densely populated rural areas and small towns
- sparsely populated rural areas with small towns and villages
- only isolated towns and villages

3. Look at the map again, and decide which of the following statements are true and which are false. Put T or F in the box beside each statement.

a. The northern hemisphere is more crowded than the southern hemisphere. **T**

b. Places near the poles are more densely populated than places near the tropics. **F**

c. Africa is more densely populated than Europe. **F**

d. Australia is more sparsely populated than Japan. **T**

e. The population of South America is evenly distributed across the continent. **F**

2.3 The population of the UK

This is about how the UK's population has changed over time.

pages 22-23

1 The Industrial Revolution saw the setting up of many factories. Imagine you are one of the child workers shown in the photograph in the student book. Write forty words describing how you feel about your work.

As well as stressing the drudgery and repetitiveness of the work some students may mention the danger of working with big machinery, especially when tired.

Tip: Remember that there may be both good and bad points – try to think of both.

2 Since 1801 the government has held a census or population count every 10 years. Before this it had no idea how many people lived in the UK. What problems do you think this may have caused for the government?

Not having a clear idea of the how large the population was must have been an obstacle to planning.

3 More of the UK population is living longer. This will bring with it some challenges for the country. These may be economic (to do with money) or social (to do with people). Think of two challenges and write your answers in the space below. An example of one of each has been done to help you.

Challenges	
Economic	Social
More money needed for pensions may make the country poorer.	More elderly people may be living on their own.
A smaller proportion of the population will be working, which means fewer people paying taxes needed for the health service.	Adults with children will also be facing the need to look after their elderly parents.
More elderly people will put a financial strain on the health service.	Older people are less mobile and can become isolated and lonely.

4 Imagine you are the Prime Minister. For one of the answers above, write down what you would do to help meet the challenge.

Answers will vary. Will their Prime Minister stress the role of the state in helping solve the problems of an ageing society, or will he/she talk about the need for more voluntary help (the 'Big Society')?

Population 13

2.4 Population around the world

This is about population growth and life expectancy around the world.

pages 24–25

1 Draw lines to match the heads and tails of these sentences.

- Population is rising fastest in Africa…
- The Earth's human population is growing at about 1.2% each year…
- Population growth is generally faster…
- …which is the poorest continent
- …the northern hemisphere
- The countries where the population is falling are found in…
- …which adds over 80 million people to Earth each year
- …in poorer less-developed countries

2 Population is growing fastest in some of the world's poorest countries. Choosing the correct words from the box, complete the paragraph below to explain why.

In poorer countries most people live by __farming__. Children are a form of __security__, as they will help on the farm and look after their parents as they become __old__. Many women do not have access to __advice__ about family life, and so many have babies one after another. Many girls have little __choice__ as they leave primary school early and are very poorly __educated__. They may be __married__ very young and they may have little say in how many children they have. Their __husbands__ are in control.

| advice | educated | married | security | choice | old | farming | husbands |

3 Low life expectancy is the result of poverty, lack of access to clean water, food and medical help. Look at the items shown in the Aid Bag below. Colour in the one that you think would be most helpful in raising life expectancy. Explain the reasons for your choice.

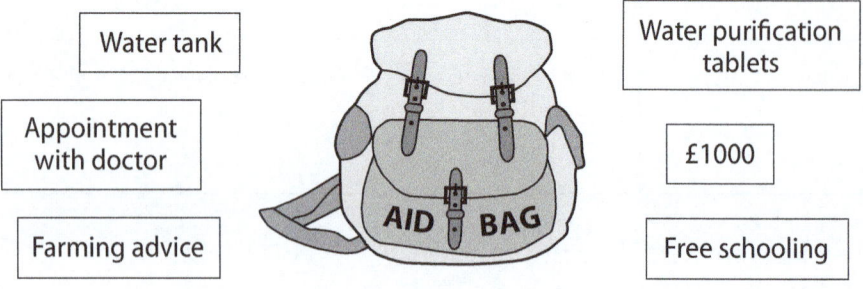

Water tank · Water purification tablets · Appointment with doctor · £1000 · Farming advice · Free schooling · AID BAG

Opinions will vary but health trumps education when it comes to simply raising life expectancy.

14 Population

2.5 Our impact on our planet

pages 26-27

This is about our increasing use of resources and what the future may be like as a result.

1 Using the information from the student book, complete the spider diagram to show how the demand for the world's resources is growing. One has been done for you.

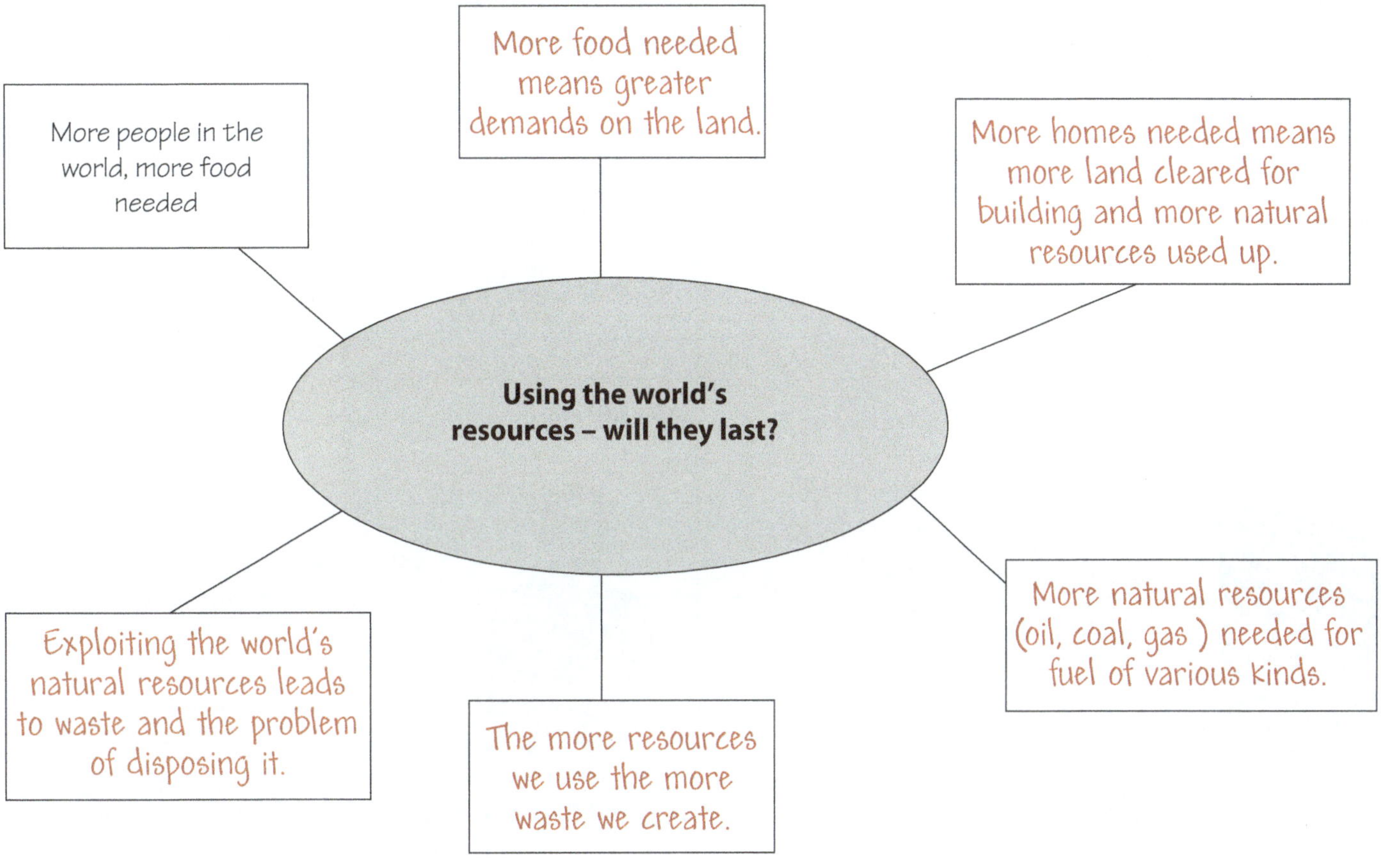

- More people in the world, more food needed
- More food needed means greater demands on the land.
- More homes needed means more land cleared for building and more natural resources used up.
- More natural resources (oil, coal, gas) needed for fuel of various kinds.
- The more resources we use the more waste we create.
- Exploiting the world's natural resources leads to waste and the problem of disposing it.

Using the world's resources – will they last?

2 We can all help the planet by living in a more sustainable way. Here are some examples.

- **A** Walk, don't drive
- **B** Recycle and re-use
- **C** Don't use plastic bags
- **D** Buy locally grown food

Choose one of the above and explain why you think it would help our planet.

Example chosen:

Explanation:

Whatever example the students choose they may pick up on the need for sustainability mentioned in the student book.

Population

2.6 What does the future hold?

This is about using evidence to plan for a growth in population.

1 The UK's population may reach 77 million by the year 2050 – that is an extra 13 million people living in the UK compared to today. How do you think this may affect our lives? Add words to the speech bubbles below to explain the effects of this population growth on each of the people and their jobs.

More doctors and nurses needed. An ageing population will put pressure on the medical profession.

Hospital Doctor

More cars and lorries on the roads. More goods may travel by road so more traffic and more congestion. But we may solve the problem in 2050 by sending more goods by train or other means of transport not even invented yet. Driverless lorries, for example, would put lorry drivers out of work.

Lorry Driver

The population will be younger than it is now, so there will be a demand for more teachers. The workforce will need to be better educated so there will be an even greater emphasis than today on achieving high standards.

Teacher

There will be even greater pressure on our national parks and similar areas for building. There will also be more visitors.

National Park warden

2 The United Nations has chosen 11 July as World Population Day, to help raise awareness of the challenges and opportunities that a rising world population will bring. The Secretary-General, Ban Ki-moon, gave this message for World Population Day on 11 July 2014.

"On this World Population Day, I call on all with influence to prioritise youth in development plans, strengthen partnerships with youth-led organisations, and involve young people in all decisions that affect them. By empowering today's youth, we will lay the groundwork for a more sustainable future for generations to come"

Do you think that young people can provide the answer to halting the growth in world population? Give reasons for your answer.

The more the next generation is aware of the problems the more chance there will be of solutions. Also, the better educated the young are, the more chance they will have smaller families.

16 Population

3 Urbanisation

pages 30-31

1. You may live in an urban area or you may have visited a nearby town or city. Circle the two words from those shown below that best describe what you think about this place. For each, give reasons for your choice.

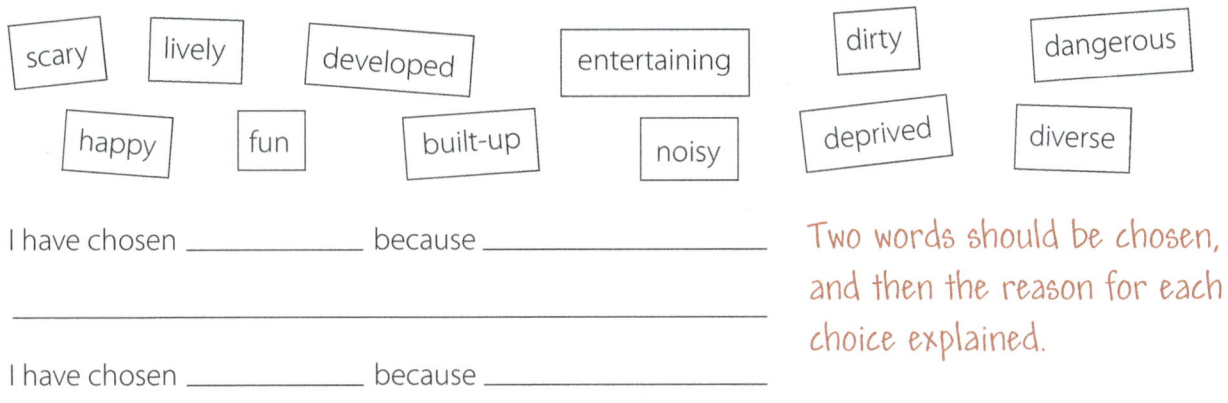

scary | lively | developed | entertaining | dirty | dangerous
happy | fun | built-up | noisy | deprived | diverse

I have chosen _____ because _____

_____

I have chosen _____ because _____

_____

Two words should be chosen, and then the reason for each choice explained.

2. Imagine that you live in the urban area shown in the photo on page 30 in the student book. You have been tweeted by a friend asking you to convince them why it would be good to move to live there. Write your reply – remember just 140 characters long, including spaces!

Tip: Be as persuasive as you can in your writing!

A piece of persuasive writing, in total just 140 characters, which encourages the person to move to the environment shown in the photograph. Answers should include reference to the facilities, services and opportunities offered in cities, and may also allude to the social aspects of city dwelling. Each part of the answer should give a positive view on city life.

3. In the space below draw a picture that shows either the advantages or disadvantages of living in an urban area.

Advantages / Disadvantages (circle one)

Accurate and well-drawn picture that reflects either the advantages/ disadvantages of living in an urban environment.

17

3.1 How our towns and cities grew

This is an exercise about the reasons behind the growth in world urbanisation.

pages 32-33

1. A list of reasons behind the growth of urbanisation is shown below, but they are in the wrong order. Put the list in the correct order, by writing a number from 1 to 7 in the correct box.

    The Industrial Revolution meant factories were built near towns so they could get workers [4]

    Some villages grew into market towns [3]

    Towns became bigger and bigger, and some became cities [7]

    Clusters of dwellings became settlements [1]

    New farm machinery, built in factories, meant that not so many farm workers were needed [5]

    Villages grew around markets [2]

    Farm workers moved to towns to find work in factories [6]

2. What are the consequences of a growth in urbanisation? Write your answers into the hexagons below. Two examples have been done for you. Try to give a balance of ideas – the consequences do not all need to be negative!

    A variety of answers are possible here, for example:
    - improved road and rail links ensure that a greater range of services and facilities are available
    - there is competition between shops and services which drives down costs
    - increasing population leads to overcrowding.

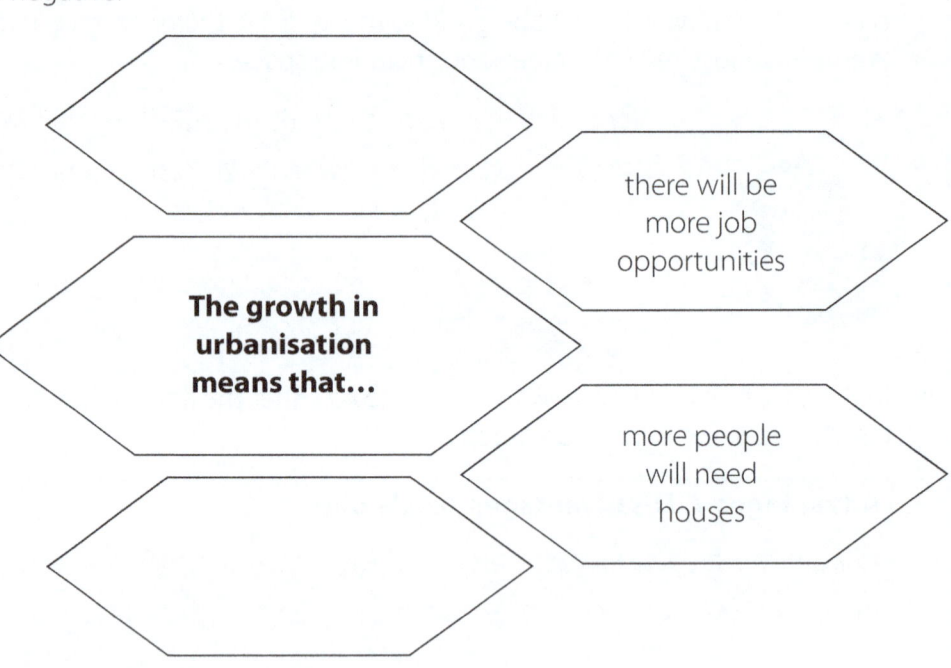

3. Now try to make links between the outer hexagons. For example, more job opportunities will mean that people may be able to afford to rent or buy housing. Compare your answers with a partner.

    Answers should begin to make links between the ideas above. For example, a greater range of services and facilities are available, but this may attract more people which, in turn, may lead to overcrowding.

18 Urbanisation

3.2 Manchester's story – part 1

This is about the early urbanisation of the city of Manchester.

1. Study the photograph below. In the spaces around the photo write down one thing that you do know about the photograph, two things that you don't know and three things that you would like to know more about.

I know …

A range of answers is possible here. All should relate in some way to the photograph stimulus.

I dont know …

I dont know …

I would like to know …

I would like to know …

I would like to know …

2. Imagine you lived in Manchester at this time, and you worked in a mill. Write about what you think your typical working day would be like? You must use the words below in your answer.

| tired | safety | painful | poor |

Answers should identify the negative working conditions of the mill employees. The paragraph should include each of the four words in the box.

Urbanisation 19

3.3 Manchester's story – part 2

This is about Manchester's more recent population changes.

pages 36-37

1. Look at the graph on page 36 in the student book. Circle the letter to show in which section of the graph – a to f – each of these statements would likely to have happened. Explain why you chose your section of the graph rather than another one.

Some shops close as the population falls   a b c (d) (e) f   d or e

Reason *As the population falls fewer people are buying from shops so some close.*

Hospitals are overcrowded   a (b) c d e f

Reason *The rapid rise in the population means more people use hospitals. This is especially true of maternity hospitals where many babies are being born.*

Thousands of new houses are built   a (b) c d e (f)   b or f

Reason *As the population rises there is a need for more housing. If the population falls, then housing may become vacant.*

Welcome to MediaCityUK, a new waterfront destination for Greater Manchester, with digital creativity, learning and leisure at its heart.

The BBC and ITV both operate at MediaCityUK, producing thousands of hours of content for television, radio and online.

Salford University also operates at MediaCityUK and says "it is a vibrant place in which to live, work, socialise and study."

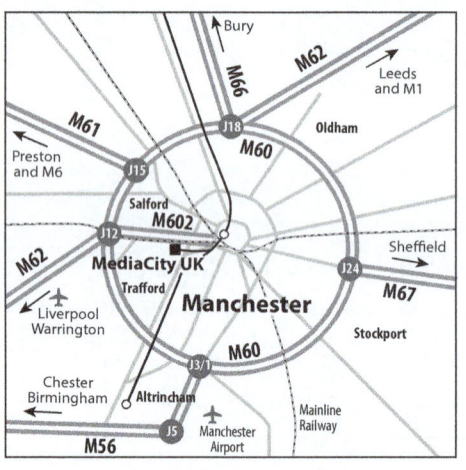

2. MediaCityUK has been developed on the Manchester Ship Canal, on the site of the docks where much of Manchester's trade was carried out. It has been said that it represents Manchester's future. How far do you agree with this statement? Give reasons for your answer below.

Student answers may focus on the positive development of new technology, media and communication industries, in contrast to Manchester's industrial past. Pupils should also offer some explanation as to why this represents the future for Manchester – many goods now being made in other countries (e.g textiles).

Urbanisation

3.4 Urbanisation around the world

This is your chance to find out about urbanisation in other countries around the world.

Over the last ten years, the number of people living in megacities with over 10 million people has increased tenfold. According to the 2011 United Nations report on world population prospects, this trend will only increase, with one out of every five people on earth expected to live in a megacity by 2025.

Rank	City	2011 population	Projected Annual Growth Rate	Estimated Population in 2025	Potential Natural Hazard
1	Lagos, Nigeria	11.2 million	3.71%	18.9 million	None
2	Dhaka, Bangladesh	15.4 million	2.84%	22.9 million	Cyclone Drought Flooding
3	Shenzhen, China	10.6 million	2.71%	15.5 million	Cyclone Drought Flooding
4	Karachi, Pakistan	13.9 million	2.68%	20.2 million	Cyclone Drought Flooding
5	Delhi, India	22.7 million	2.67%	32.9 million	Drought Flooding

1 The United Nations report that most of these cities are also at risk from natural hazards. Use an atlas to locate the five cities in the table above on the world map below. The, write a letter to the United Nations explaining why the expected population growth in these cities may cause problems.

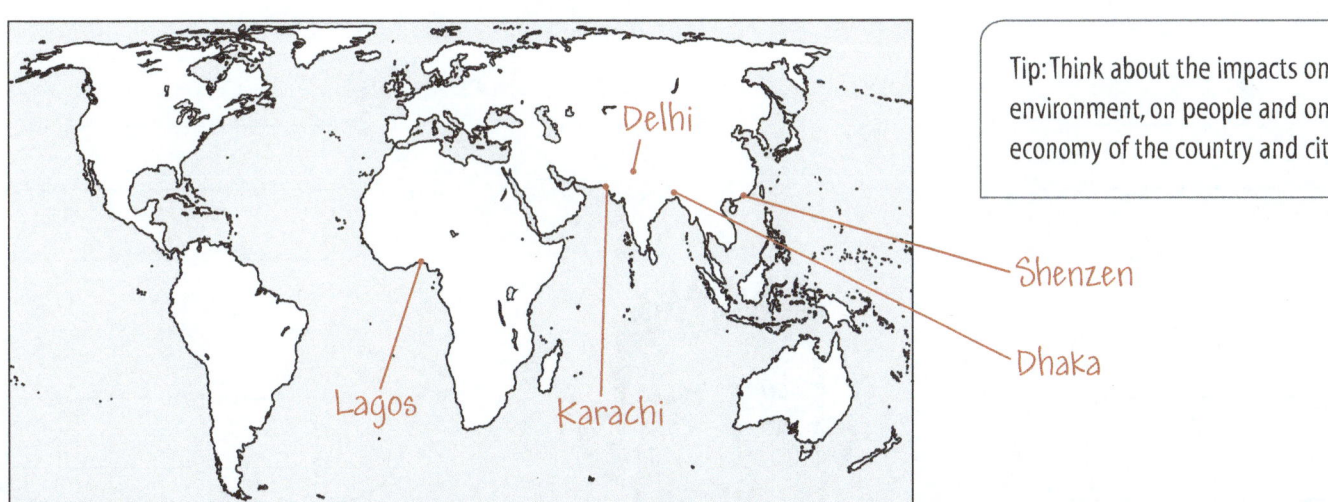

Tip: Think about the impacts on the environment, on people and on the economy of the country and city.

The letter should make direct links between population growth and the natural hazards identified. For example, as the population in Dhaka grows, more people will be at risk from flooding, which is likely to lead to more loss of life.

Urbanisation

3.5 Why do people move to urban areas?

This is where you will discover the reasons why people move from the countryside to cities.

pages 40-41

1. Think about your own life. Write down three reasons why you might choose to move to another town, city or country in the future. Explain, for each, whether it would be caused by a push or pull factor.

	Reason for moving	Push / Pull	Explanation
1			All answers should give a reason (R), identify push or pull (P), and then offer some explanation (E). A range of ideas possible, some reasons may include: to change job (R), pull (P) to earn more money (E), to move away from crime (R), push (P) to improve quality of life (E) to retire to the seaside (R), pull (P), for a quieter life (R).
2			
3			

2. For each of your own reasons above, describe one change to your own area that would mean that you would not be tempted to move.

Reasons given should relate to those given above, e.g. change of job; better employment opportunities available locally; crime; improve the safety of the area by installing better lighting along roads; retire; develop more green and open spaces for people to enjoy.

22 Urbanisation

3.6 It's not all sunshine!

This is where you will discover whether you would be suited to city life.

pages 42-43

1. Page 42 of the student book shows some of the benefits and disadvantages of city life. Choose any three of each and list them below.

Benefits of city life	Disadvantages of city life

Benefits should be taken from the first photo: lots to do, concerts, being close to people with similar interests, interesting mix of people, choice in food, services and jobs, and good transport links.

Disadvantages from the second photo could include air pollution, a sense of isolation, higher living costs, a very busy environment and the possibility of more crime.

2. In the space below design an area of a city where you would like to live. It should have each of your chosen benefits, but also should have some design features that mean the disadvantages are no longer a problem!

Tip: Think as creatively as you can and give your city an appropriate name!

Chosen benefits identified in question 1 should be reproduced in the design shown here. The disadvantages shown in question 1 should have measures put in place to minimise them, e.g. only electric cars allowed, affordable housing schemes, a range of social activities to help bring people together.

Urbanisation 23

3.7 Life in the slums

This is where you will find out about the poorest people who live in cities.

1. The paragraph below describes life in the slums.

   Circle the correct word from each pair. Use page 44 in the student book to help you.

   Cities are growing **(fast)** / **slow** in developing countries. Many slums are made from anything the people can find, and have **(no)** / **some** running water. Around **half** / **(one-third)** of people in developing countries live in slums. That is **(860)** / **86** million people in all. Osakwe lives in a slum in **Lisbon** / **(Lagos)**. Nine people live in **(two)** / **four** rooms, so it is very crowded. There is a lot of rubbish, and people throw it into the **(ditch)** / **bins** outside the house.

2. Look at the photographs of the slums in the student book. Choose three adjectives to describe what they are like. One adjective should have 4 letters, one should have 6 with the last having 8 letters.

   Adjective 1 (4 letters) Words such as drab, dour, poor and ugly   **Adjective 2** (6 letters) Words such as broken, dreary, earthy, untidy   **Adjective 3** (8 letters) Words such as dreadful, battered, shocking and terrib[le]

3. One way to tackle the slum problem is through self-help schemes, and many British charities support these. Save the Children, a British charity, set up in 1919, also say that:

   'Education is many children's route out of poverty. It gives them a chance to gain valuable knowledge and skills, and to improve their lives. And it means when they grow up, their children will have a much better chance of surviving and thriving.'

   If you were making the decision on how to spend £5 million to help people like Osakwe in the slums of Lagos, would you spend it on schools and teachers, or building materials for houses? You have a difficult choice.
   Write a letter to the Nigerian government explaining your decision.

   Students should identify how they would spend the money and give reasons explaining their choice. Either choice is acceptable as long as clear reasons are given.
   Possible reasons may be:
   Schools: if young people get educated they will have a better chance of getting themselves out of poverty by gaining employment; the development of schools will help to raise aspirations; schools can be used to educate people about self-help, sustainable schemes.
   Building materials: this will have quite an immediate impact as people will have access to improved housing; this will improve their lives and help raise their self-esteem; residents may feel better about themselves and feel more motivated to further improve their lives.

Urbanisation

3.8 A city of the future?

This is where you can display your creativity!

pages 46–47

1 Masdar City aims to be the world's most sustainable city. The Abu Dhabi royal family want the world to know about it and have asked you to create an eye-catching poster to tell the world. The six aims are shown below but you have also been asked to think of two other aims that you think should form part of this exciting project. Draw pictures in the spaces below to create your poster, and don't forget to add your own special sustainable aims at the end!

Avoid fossil fuels	Keep cool
The poster should be informative and eye-catching. The diagrams should clearly represent the six aims. Students should further consider two other aims of their own choice (such as to educate its people or to be a world-leader in design for example) that they think would be appropriate.	
Be walkable	**Allow high population density**
Have car-free streets	**Minimise waste**
_____	_____

Urbanisation 25

4 Coasts

pages 48-49

1. What does a coast mean to you? In the space below draw a picture of a coastal scene. If you live on the coast, it could be where you live. Or perhaps a scene you remember from a holiday? Or it could be an imaginary coast anywhere in the world. Add labels or text to your drawing if you want to.

> Answers will vary. The question has been framed so that all students should be able to answer it, even if they have never been to a coast.

2. Write down two things you know about coasts.

   a _____

   b _____

3. Write down two things you would like to know about coasts.

   a _____

   b _____

4. At the end of this topic, come back and see if you've found out about these things If you have, draw a ☺ next to your question - if you haven't, draw a ☹!

26

4.1 Waves and tides

This is about what causes the waves and tides, and the different types of waves.

geog.2
pages 50-51

1 Choose words from the box to fill in the gaps in the sentences below.

| sun | weak | boats | wind | moon | big | small | long |
| backwash | short | fetch | carry | strong | swash |

Waves are made by _wind_ pulling on the surface of the water.

The length of water over which the wind blows is called the _fetch_ .

Large waves are made by:

✓ _strong_ wind

✓ the wind blowing for a _long_ time

✓ a _big_ fetch

The water that goes up the beach when a wave breaks is called the _swash_ .

The water that goes back down the beach is called the _backwash_ .

Tides are caused by the pull of the _moon_ .

2 Write the correct caption from the bullet list below underneath each diagram of a wave.

- If a wave is high and steep, it erodes the beach.
- If a wave is high and steep, it builds up the beach.
- If a wave is low and flat, it erodes the beach.
- If a wave is low and flat, it builds up the beach.

If a wave is high and steep, it erodes the beach.

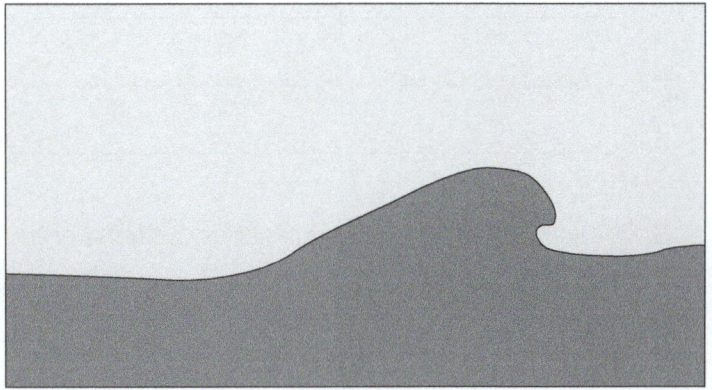

If a wave is low and flat, it builds up the beach.

Coasts 27

4.2 The waves at work

This is about what jobs waves do.

pages 52-53

1 Write these phrases into the correct part of the table below.

- the process is called longshore drift
- how the waves wear away the coast
- a beach is made like this
- when waves drop the load they are carrying
- low flat waves drop material
- material is moved in a zig-zag by the swash and the backwash
- the four processes are called solution, hydraulic action, attrition and abrasion
- when material is carried along the coast

erosion	transport	deposition
how the waves wear away the coast the four processes are called solution, hydraulic action, attrition and abrasion	the process is called longshore drift material is moved in a zig-zag by the swash and the backwash when material is carried along the coast	a beach is made like this when waves drop the load they are carrying low flat waves drop material

2 Which process do you think needs the **most** energy? Why?

Erosion, because this process involves the breaking down of rock.

3 Which process do you think needs the **least** energy? Why?

Deposition, because it is the end result of the transport process.

28 Coasts

4.3 Landforms created by the waves

This is about how coastal landforms are made.

1. The diagram below shows several coastal landforms. Add the labels from the box to it.

- crack
- cave
- stack
- wave-cut platform

2. Explain how waves have created the landforms in the diagram.

   By eroding rocks of differing hardness and then transporting and depositing the eroded material.

3. What do you think will happen to these landforms next? Why?

   The cave will become an arch, the stack will fall into the sea and the crack will widen and cause another fall into the sea, creating a new stack.

   Draw a diagram of your prediction here:

Coasts 29

4.4 The coast and us

This is about how the coast is used in many ways by different groups of people.

Natural
This is about the environment – energy, air, water, soil, living things.

Who decides
This is about who makes choices and decides what is to happen.

Economic
This is about money, trade, buying and selling.

Social
This is about people and the way they live their lives.

To help you remember these four points, think; **N**orth, **E**ast, **S**outh, **W**est.

1 Look carefully at the photo above and the four 'points of the compass' around it.

Write down how people may affect the coastline in natural, economic and social ways.

Natural
By building sea defences and channels along the coast and in estuaries thus changing the course of the waves and the rivers.

Economic
By building harbours and port facilities (warehouses etc.)

Social
Recreational activities along the coast and in estuaries can affect the shape of the coast.

2 Choose one of your three answers.

Write in more detail about how people may have good or bad effects on the coast.

Natural / Economic / Social (circle your choice)

The good effects are likely to be mainly natural, where we make efforts to preserve wildlife areas. Good and bad effects, which are dealt with on pages 56 and 57 of the student book, are largely economic and social.

Coasts

4.5 Your holiday in Newquay

This is about using an OS map to find out more about Newquay.

1. In the spaces below, fill in details for an information leaflet for tourists who want to visit Newquay. Look at the OS map on page 23 of the student book to help you.

Newquay in Cornwall
A holiday for all ages!

Beaches — Beaches include Fistral, Crantock, Watergate, Beacon Cove and New Bay.

Countryside — The surrounding countryside can be reached by many footpaths including the south-west coastal path and cycle paths.

Things to do — Things to do include surfing, sailing, walking cycling and fishing (at sea or in the Porth Reservoir).

2. You could travel to Newquay by road, rail or air.
   Choose how you would travel to Newquay and explain why.
   Is your chosen method sustainable?

   I would travel to Newquay by road / rail / air (circle your choice)
   I would travel this way because

   Answers will vary, but rail may be the responsible choice, as 100 000 visitors would bring a lot of cars with them to such a small town. On the other hand, a car is the best way of transporting your surfboard!

Coasts 31

4.6 Under threat from the sea

The floods of the winter of 2013-2014 had a major impact on the country. Can you remember what happened?

Were you or where you live affected by the floods during the winter of 2013/2014? If so, write an account of what happened to you or to other people where you live. If you were not directly affected, write an account of what you saw on the TV, heard about through social media or read in the newspapers. You will find plenty of information to remind you on the internet.

Answers will vary. Memories of the 2013/14 storms should be fresh in most students' minds.

4.7 How long can Happisburgh hang on?

This is about how one village is falling into the sea!

pages 62-63

1. The boxes on the right explain why the village is falling into the sea. But they are in the wrong order! Write the correct order in the circles.

2. This diagram shows what is happening. Label:

   groynes   revetments   cliff
   houses at risk   beach

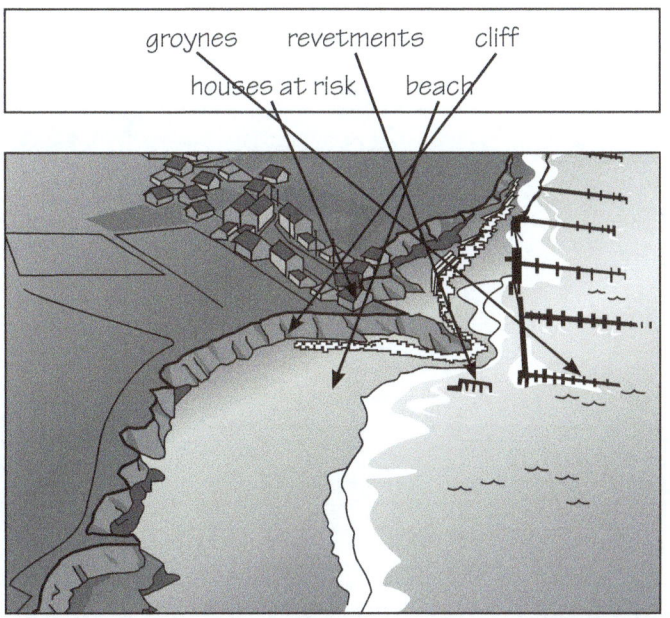

> The clay slides out of the bottom of the cliff and the sand on top collapses. ⑤
>
> All the time, the sea is also taking chunks out of the bottom of the cliffs by wave erosion. ④
>
> The cliffs are sand on top of clay below. ①
>
> The clay gets wet and the water makes it slippery. ③
>
> Rain can get through the sand to the clay. ②

3. The people whose homes are destroyed can't get the money from insurance. Cliff falls are called 'Acts of God' and aren't covered by insurance.

   a How do you think the people feel about this? Why?

   Resentful is the likely answer — because their houses are valuable to them. But some students may mention that they knew that they were not insurable when they bought their houses!

   b Do you think they should get compensation? Why/why not? (Think about everyone else's insurance premiums, the amount taxes might go up, whether it's fair ...)

   Answers will vary. Some students may make a comparison with houses in flood prone areas having to pay more insurance — at least they are covered. So there is an argument that cover should be offered, even if it would be much higher than the average.

Coasts 33

4.8 Protecting places from the sea

This is about how planners are trying to prevent erosion at the coast.

1 The pictures below show ways to reduce erosion.

   a For each one, write a title at the top. Choose from:
      Sea wall, Wave-break, Beach replenishment, Groynes, Pipes, Rock armour.

1 **Sea Wall**

These stop the waves reaching valuable land.

2 **Rock armour**

These soak up the energy of the waves.

3 **Wave-break (or Reef)**

These make the waves break away from the beach.

4 **Groynes**

These stop the sand being carried away and absorb some of the waves' energy.

5 **Beach replenishment**

(or Nourishment) This builds up the beach.

6 **Pipes**

(not shown in student book) These prevent cliff erosion by draining water from the cliffs.

   b Underneath each picture explain how the method works.

   c Which method do you think is most effective? Why?

   Answers will vary. It is clear that sea walls are by far the most expensive and therefore only possible in few places. Students may point out that cost effectiveness is a significant criterion.

   d Which one do you think is least effective? Why?

   Answers will vary. Possibly sea walls for reasons of cost; possibly wooden revetments and groynes, as students can see from the Happisburgh example that they didn't do much to save the houses there

34 Coasts

5 Weather and climate

pages 66-67

1. What is the climate like where you live?

   What are the good things about it and what are the bad things?

   Good things

   _____

   _____

   _____

   _____

   _____

   Bad things

   _____

   _____

   _____

   _____

   _____

   Being made to think about the good things about our climate will act as a counterweight to our normal habit of running our climate down!

2. How do you rate your climate?

   Rate your climate for the following factors on a scale of 1 to 10. (1 means you think there's too little of it, 10 means you think there's too much). Then compare your decisions with those of your friends. Discuss the reasons for your ratings.

   Rain

   1 2 3 4 5 6 7 8 9 10
   ☐ ☐ ☐ ☐ ☐ ☐ ☐ ☐ ☐ ☐

   Sun

   1 2 3 4 5 6 7 8 9 10
   ☐ ☐ ☐ ☐ ☐ ☐ ☐ ☐ ☐ ☐

   Wind

   1 2 3 4 5 6 7 8 9 10
   ☐ ☐ ☐ ☐ ☐ ☐ ☐ ☐ ☐ ☐

   The definition in the student book is;
   Weather is the state of the atmosphere in a place.

   Some students may look for further definitions and note that weather is the current situation rather than an average over time.
   This exercise will benefit from a group discussion about our climate. Those with knowledge of other countries may bring their experience to bear. It's no accident that the word 'temperate' is used to describe our climate.

3. Imagine if the climate was the same all over the world. What impact would this have on the way we all live?

   Some students may say that it depends on what that 'same' climate was! And they would be right. But the intention of the exercise is to stimulate the students' imagination. For example, why go on summer holidays if the weather is the same everywhere? And we would all grow and eat the same sorts of fruit and vegetables, so no more exotic food!

5.1 It's the weather!

pages 68-69

This is about how the weather affects different people and you!

1. Add words to the speech bubbles to explain how different types of weather could affect the following people.

Lorry driver

Ideas include:
Bad weather – snow and flooding – affects delivery times and has an impact on the economy. It can be very dangerous driving in bad weather. Really hot weather can damage some cargoes (e.g. live animals).

Farmer

Farmers are the group most affected by weather conditions. Extremes of all kinds can damage crops or affect yields. Animals can suffer in unexpected bad weather (e.g. snowstorms) and in times of drought.

Hotel owner

Hotel bookings can be hit by bad weather, particularly in the summer holiday season. A good summer in the UK can mean more bookings as people decide to take a 'staycation'.

Supermarket manager

A bad harvest or poor yields of fresh fruit and vegetables can affect prices in the supermarket. Intense competition means prices may be held down at the expense of profits.

2. Think about how the weather affects you. Sometimes it is fun, and sometimes it is not! Write about one way that the weather has affected you.

Type of weather   Answers will vary.

36   Weather and climate

5.2 So what causes weather?

This is about the main causes of weather.

pages 70-71

1 Look at the picture below which shows the two main ways that weather can be caused.
   A Key Stage 2 teacher has asked you to write an explanation for her class of nine year olds.
   Write your explanations in the boxes below using page 70 of the student book to help you.
   Add pictures if it would help them to understand!

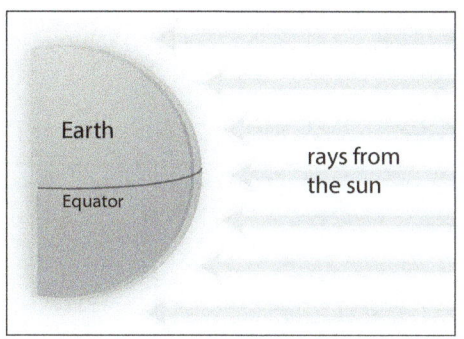

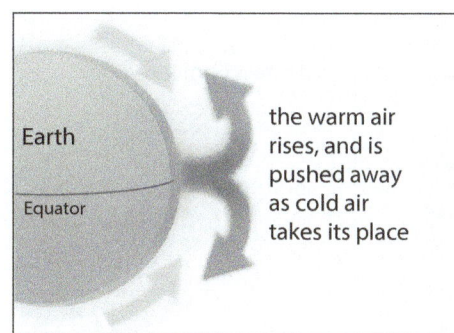

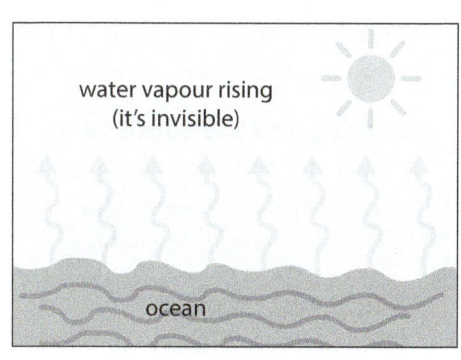

The Sun heats Earth. But it does not heat it *evenly*, because Earth is round. The top and bottom don't warm up much.

Earth in turn heats the air. The warm air rises. Air from a colder place then flows in to replace it, as **wind**. (Wind is just air on the move.)

The Sun also warms the oceans. This causes water to evaporate to give off a gas, **water vapour**. That gas plays a big part in the weather.

2 Fill in the gaps in this paragraph about water vapour. Choose words from this list

   | evaporate grass hang condense gas dew |

Water vapour is a __gas__ . In cold weather it may __condense__ around us as fog, or it may __hang__ in the air as mist. Sometimes it condenses on cold __grass__ and leaves and becomes __dew__ . When the sun shines, all of these __evaporate__ again.

Weather and climate 37

5.3 Measuring the weather

This is about mapping the weather, and how it is measured.

pages 72-73

1. What is weather? Write your definition here. The definition in the student book is;

   Weather is the state of the atmosphere in a place. Some students may look for further definitions and note that weather is the current situation rather than an average over time.

2. Read the weather descriptions below for four areas of the UK. Then look at the weather symbols box. Draw the correct weather symbols in the boxes on the map to match the description of the weather in that area.

   London and the South East
   Mainly dry and bright with spells of sunshine, but also risk of showers. Maximum 9 °C. 5 mph south-westerly winds.

   Southwest England
   Long periods of heavy rain. Maximum 8 °C. 10 mph westerly winds.

   Northwest England
   Cloudy with risk of showers. Maximum 7 °C. 5 mph westerly winds.

   Northeast Scotland
   Dry and bright. Maximum 8 °C. 10 mph south-westerly winds.

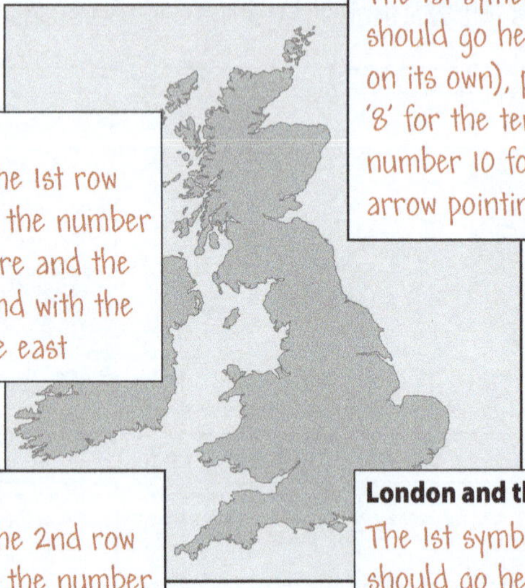

   North east Scotland
   The 1st symbol in the 2nd row should go here (or just the sun on its own), plus the number '8' for the temperature and the number 10 for the wind with the arrow pointing to the north east

   Northwest England
   The 2nd symbol in the 1st row should go here, plus the number '7' for the temperature and the number 5 for the wind with the arrow pointing to the east

   Southwest England
   The 2nd symbol in the 2nd row should go here, plus the number '8' for the temperature and the number 10 for the wind with the arrow pointing to the east

   London and the South East
   The 1st symbol in the 2nd row should go here, plus the number '9' for the temperature and the number 5 for the wind with the arrow pointing to the north east

        (27) (The figure in the circle is the wind speed. The arrow shows the direction of the wind.)

   16 (Use numbers for temperature.)

3. Put a ring round the odd one out in each set below. Explain your choice of odd one out.

   a. °C   millibars   (wind speed)   oktas

   Explanation: Wind speed is a description but not a unit of measurement.

   b. temperature   (thermometer)   precipitation   cloud cover

   Explanation: A thermometer is an object for measuring while the other terms are descriptions.

   c. anemometer   barometer   rain gauge   (km/h)

   Explanation: Km/h is a unit of measurement while the others are means of making measurements.

   d. (sun)   snow   drizzle   rain

   Explanation: All except the sun are different kinds of precipitation.

38 Weather and climate

5.4 More about rain … and clouds

This is about three types of rainfall.

pages 74-75

1 These pictures show three different types of rainfall. Write the text beside each picture in the correct box on the picture.

Convectional rainfall

The rising air cools. The water vapour condenses. Clouds form. It rains.

The sun warms the ground … which then warms the air above it.

Currents of warm air rise.

3 The rising air cools. The water vapour condenses. Clouds form. It rains.

2 Currents of warm air rise.

1 The sun warms the ground … which then warms the air above it.

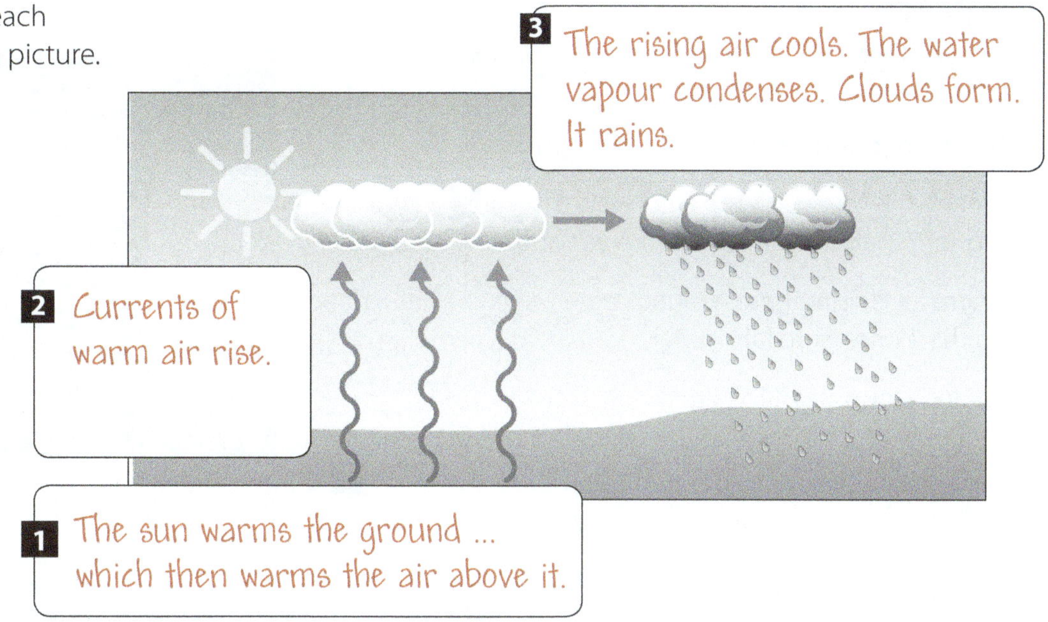

Relief rainfall

The rising air cools. The water vapour condenses. Clouds form. It rains.

Warm moist air arrives from the Atlantic Ocean.

The rain falls on the windward side of the mountain. The leeward side stays dry.

The air is forced to rise.

3 The rising air cools. The water vapour condenses. Clouds form. It rains.

2 The air is forced to rise.

1 Warm moist air arrives from the Atlantic Ocean.

4 The rain falls on the windward side of the mountain. The leeward side stays dry.

leeward (sheltered)

windward (facing the wind)

Frontal rainfall

The warm air mass slides up over the cold one, or gets driven up by it.

A warm air mass meets a cold air mass.

The rising air cools. The water vapour condenses. Clouds form. It rains.

warm

2 The warm air mass slides up over the cold one, or gets driven up by it.

1 A warm air mass meets a cold air mass.

3 The rising air cools. The water vapour condenses. Clouds form. It rains.

cold

Weather and climate 39

5.5 Air pressure

This is about the weather you get with high and low air pressure.

pages 76-77

1. The pictures show low and high pressure weather. Write the text below in the correct box on each picture, then complete the sentences underneath.

But warm rising air means clouds form …

Meanwhile, over at B the air pressure is higher. So air rushes from B to A as wind.

Warm air is rising here, around A. So the air pressure falls at A.

… and clouds lead to rain.

A fall in air pressure is a sign of ___wind___ and ___rain___ .

The lower the ___pressure___ the worse the ___weather___ will be.

… and far away, at Y, it sinks. This causes the air pressure at Y to rise.

… so cold air gets pushed aside …

Now Y has high pressure.

Warm air is rising at X …

As the cold air sinks it warms up. So no water vapour condenses and no clouds form over Y. The sky stays clear.

High pressure means no ___clouds___.

It gives our hottest ___summer___ weather and ___our coldest___ winter weather.

Low pressure weather

2. Meanwhile, over at B the air pressure is higher. So air rushes from B to A as wind.

3. But warm rising air means clouds form …

1. Warm air is rising here, around A. So the air pressure falls at A.

4. … and clouds lead to rain.

High pressure weather

2. … so cold air gets pushed aside …

3. … and far away, at Y, it sinks. This causes the air pressure at Y to rise.

4. As the cold air sinks it warms up. So no water vapour condenses and no clouds form over Y. The sky stays clear.

1. Warm air is rising at X …

5. Now Y has high pressure.

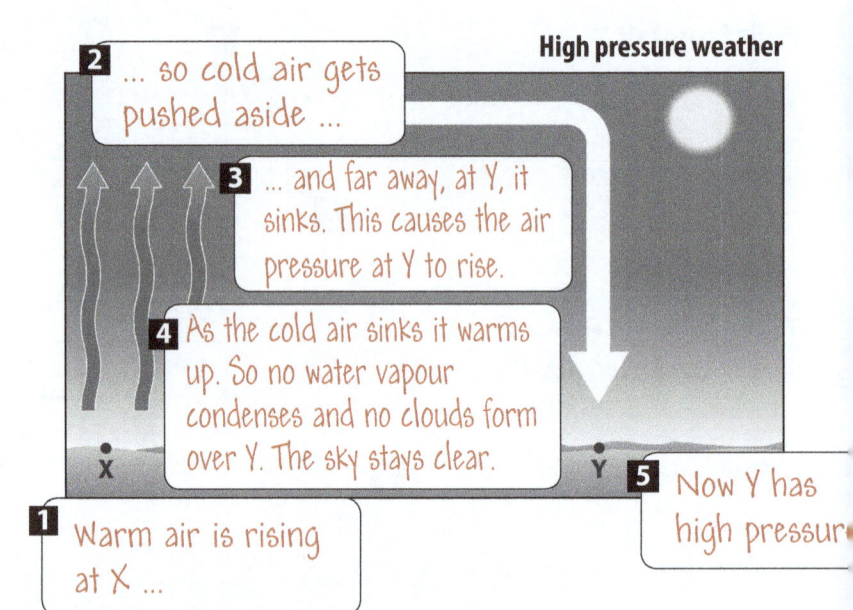

2. Describe the weather you get with high pressure in winter and summer. You need to mention whether there are any clouds, whether it is hot or cold, and whether there is any rain. Make sure you also include the words in the box.

| frost dew thunderstorms fog drought flooding |

In the summer high pressure means that it can be cold at night so that water vapour condenses as dew. No cloud means no rain so there is a danger of drought. As the air rises, thunderstorms can develop which can lead to flooding. In the winter water vapour can condense on cold surfaces and then freeze, giving frost, or it can condense on dust and other particles in the air, leading to fog.

5.6 Why is our weather so changeable?

This is about why our weather in the UK changes so quickly.

pages 78-79

1 Are these statements true or false? Put a tick in the correct box.

		True	False
a	The air moves around the world in huge blocks called air masses.	✓	
b	A warm air mass brings strong gusty wind and heavy rain.		✓
c	An air mass coming from the North Pole will be warm and damp.		✓
d	The leading edge of an air mass is called a front.	✓	
e	A cold air mass brings wind and rain.		✓
f	When a new air mass reaches the UK, it brings a change in the weather.	✓	
g	An air mass coming from a warm ocean will be cold and dry.		✓
h	Warm air always moves from a warmer place to a colder one.	✓	
i	The UK is closer to the equator than to the north pole.		✓

2 The diagram below right shows what happens when a warm air mass arrives. The text below explains what happens – but it is in the wrong order. Put it in the right order by writing numbers 1–4 next to it.

[2] The rising air cools. The water vapour condenses to form a sloping bank of cloud.

[1] Warm air is lighter. So it slides up over the cold air.

[4] It starts to rain. It may rain for hours.

[3] As it rises, the pressure falls. So the weather gets a bit windy.

3 Draw the weather symbol for; *The symbols are shown on page 79 of the student book.*

a A warm front

b A cold front

Finish the sentences.

A warm front means *a warm air mass is arriving.*

A cold front means *a cold air mass is arriving.*

Weather and climate 41

5.7 A winter of storms

This is about storms that can badly affect the UK.

1. You work on a newspaper and have been asked to write about how storms affect the UK.
   Fill in the spaces below and give your story a catchy headline at the top.

Students will use the information on pages 80-81 in the student book. Or they may research on the internet.

The storm was caused…

People and places were affected in many different ways.

42   Weather and climate

.8 From weather to climate

This is about climate and climate graphs.

pages 82-83

1 Complete the following statements.

Climate is … *the average weather in a place.*

Climate is worked out by … *taking daily measurements over a long period.*

A climate graph shows … *the average temperatures and rainfall for a place over the year.*

2 The map shows the four climate regions for the UK. Below it is a climate graph for one place in each region.

a Complete the table using information from the graphs.

	Oban	Aviemore	Penzance	Margate
Jan temp °C	4	1	7	4
July temp °C	15	13	17	18
Jan rainfall mm	140	90	120	50
July rainfall mm	125	65	70	55
Total rainfall	1400	850	1050	600

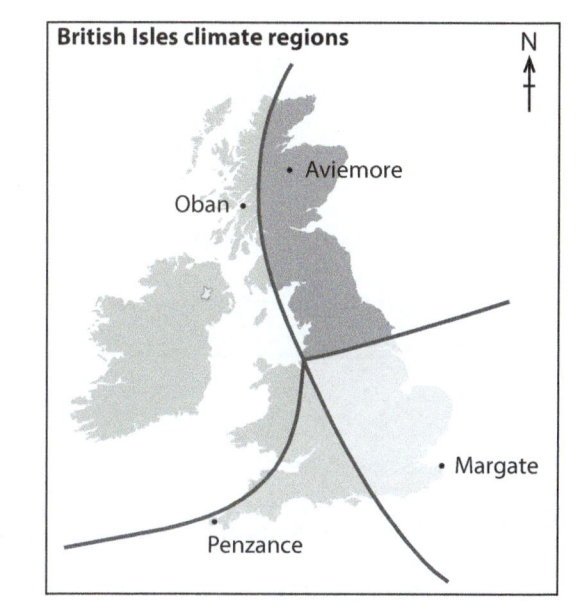

British Isles climate regions

- Aviemore
- Oban
- Margate
- Penzance

b Choose two of the locations from the map. Say which ones you have chosen and describe what the weather will be like in winter and summer in those two places. Use information from the table above and the climate graphs to help you.

The comparison would be most useful if students chose one west coast station and one other station (Aviemore or Margate).

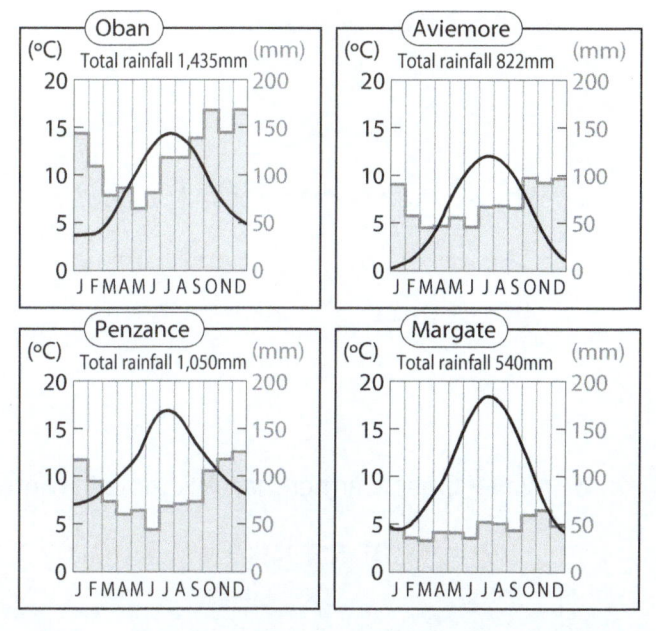

Oban — Total rainfall 1,435mm
Aviemore — Total rainfall 822mm
Penzance — Total rainfall 1,050mm
Margate — Total rainfall 540mm

Note Aviemore is 230 m above sea level. All the other locations lie at sea level.

Weather and climate **43**

5.9 The factors that influence climate

This is about why climate is different in different places.

1 Draw a line to match each factor affecting climate with the correct effect below.

Factors	Effects
Latitude	In the UK, the North Atlantic drift warms the west coast in winter.
Distance from the coast	The further you go from the equator the cooler it gets.
Prevailing wind direction	A sea breeze keeps the coast cool in summer and warm in winter.
Ocean currents	In the UK, it's from the south west and brings rain.
Height above sea level/altitude	The higher you are above sea level the cooler it is.

Matches:
- Latitude → The further you go from the equator the cooler it gets.
- Distance from the coast → A sea breeze keeps the coast cool in summer and warm in winter.
- Prevailing wind direction → In the UK, it's from the south west and brings rain.
- Ocean currents → In the UK, the North Atlantic drift warms the west coast in winter.
- Height above sea level/altitude → The higher you are above sea level the cooler it is.

2 Look at the map and answer the questions.

a Why is Margate always warmer than Aviemore?

Margate is further south and lies at sea level.

b Why will Leicester be warmer than Margate in summer, but cooler in winter?

Leicester lies inland away from the coast with its moderating winds.

c Why is Penzance wetter than Margate?

The prevailing wind comes straight in from the sea, bringing rain, whereas the rain has lessened by the time it reaches Margate on the east coast.

d Why is Oban warmer than Aviemore in winter?

Oban lies at sea level and is warmed by the North Atlantic drift.

Weather and climate

10 Climates around the world

This is about climate in different parts of the world.

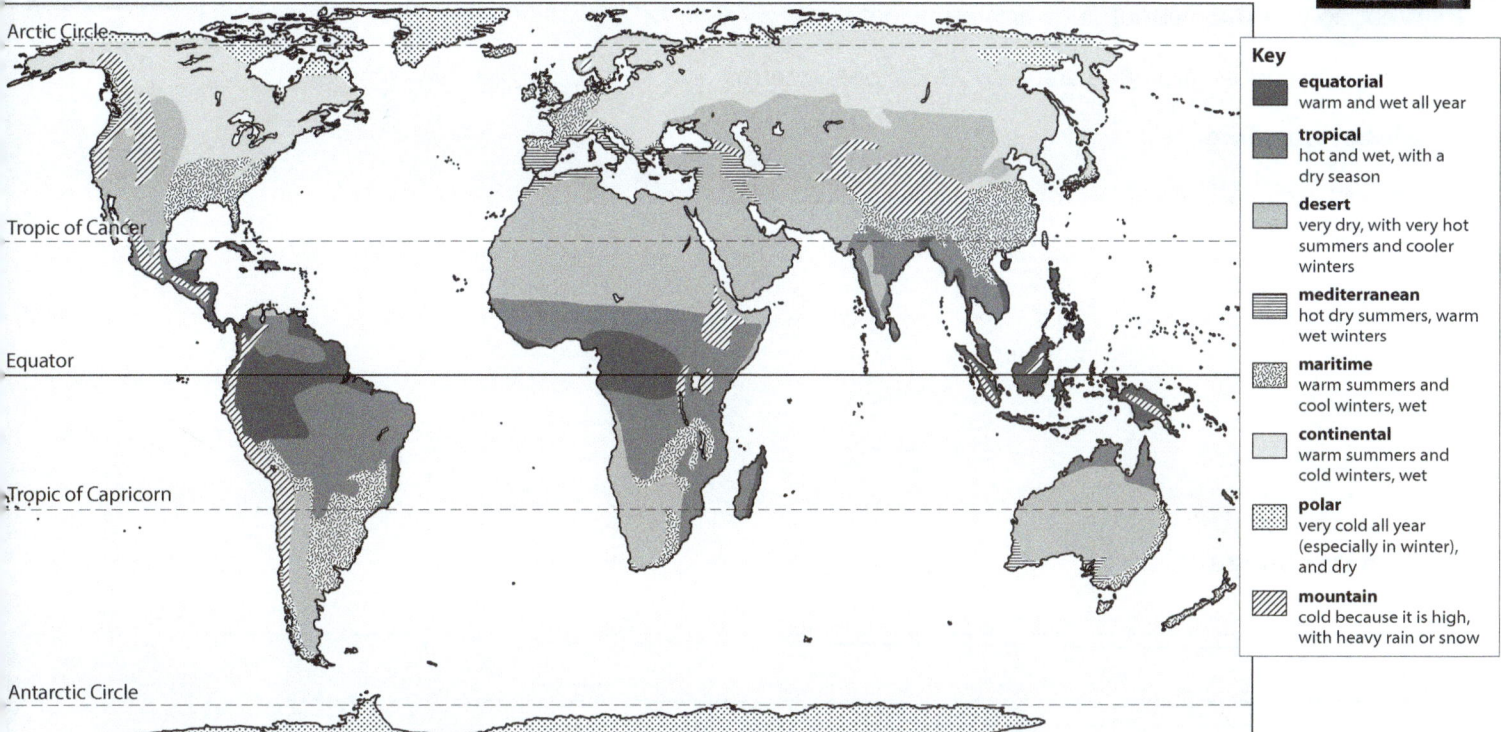

geog.2
pages 86-87

Key
- **equatorial** warm and wet all year
- **tropical** hot and wet, with a dry season
- **desert** very dry, with very hot summers and cooler winters
- **mediterranean** hot dry summers, warm wet winters
- **maritime** warm summers and cool winters, wet
- **continental** warm summers and cold winters, wet
- **polar** very cold all year (especially in winter), and dry
- **mountain** cold because it is high, with heavy rain or snow

1 The map shows how the climate varies across the globe.
Choose one of the climates where you would like to go on holiday to. Explain why.

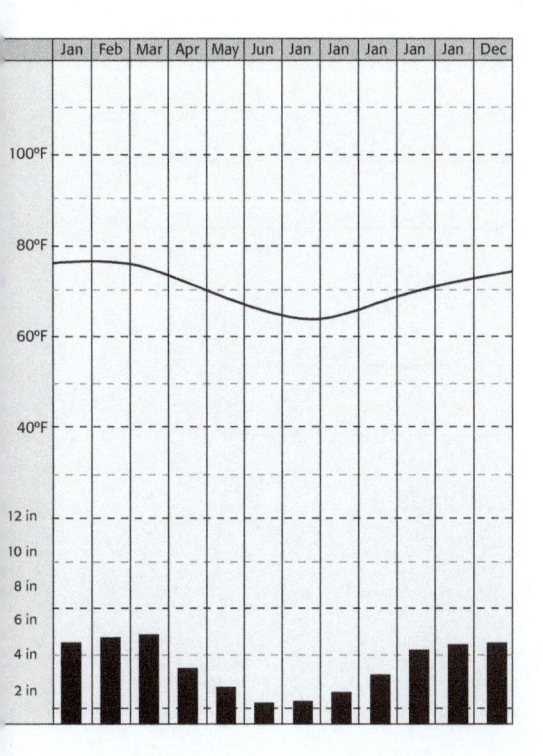

Name of climate _Answers will vary._

2 Look at this climate graph for Durban in South Africa. Compare the climate of Durban with that of London. Use the graph on page 83 of the student book to help you and use numbers/figures from the graphs to help your answer.

Temperature First the students will have to convert the figures from Fahrenheit and inches to centigrade and millimetres!

Rainfall Then they should mention the greater variability of London's temperature due to its higher latitude and the different seasonality as Durban is in the southern hemisphere. Durban is noticeably wetter, due to prevailing winds.

Weather and climate **45**

6 Our warming planet

geog.2
pages 88-89

1. What do you know about our warming planet?

   Write down what you understand by the following terms:

   Global warming

   Answers will vary. Some students may already have a clear idea of what is meant by these terms; others will be more confused as to the relationship between them.

   Climate change

   _____
   _____
   _____
   _____
   _____

   Emissions

   _____
   _____
   _____
   _____
   _____

2. At the end of this topic, come back and see if you were right about these things If you were, draw a ☺ next to what you have written - if you haven't, draw a ☹!

1 Earth's temperature through the ages

Here you will learn more about three periods in our history when the climate was different from today.

geog.2
pages 90-91

Roman Britain was warmer that it is today. Find out how the warm climate helped the Romans to settle Britain, as well as growing grapes.

Students will find plenty of information on the internet under headings such as:
'Roman warm period', 'Viking settlement of Greenland', 'Little Ice Age', and 'River Thames Frost Fair'.

Find out more about how the Vikings settled Greenland, including the story of how it got its name!

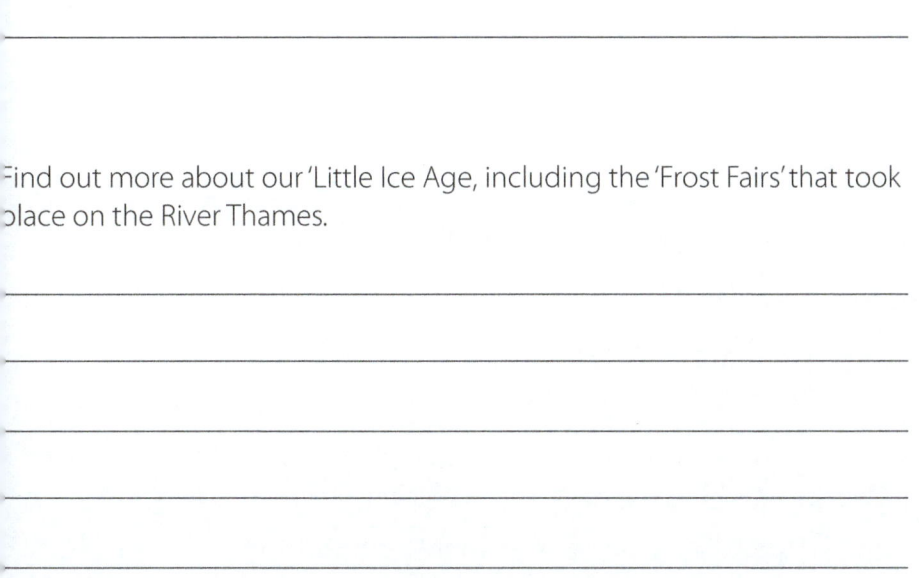

_____
_____
_____
_____
_____

Find out more about our 'Little Ice Age, including the 'Frost Fairs' that took place on the River Thames.

_____
_____
_____
_____
_____

Our warming planet 47

6.2 Global warming

This is about the reasons behind global warming.

pages 92-93

'The data proves it's mostly our fault'

'We are damaging our planet for the future'

'Some people say it's our fault, others say it is a natural event. I'm confused.'

'I need my car. How am I supposed to work without it?'

1 Look at what the people are saying above. Give one reason why they have that point of view.

Scientist

The scientist works with facts and these indicate that humans are at least partly responsible for the current trend in global warming.

Environmentalist

The environmentalist is concerned about the impact that we are having on wildlife, for which there is plenty of evidence. Global warming is one aspect of that impact.

Pupil

The media has tended to give fairly even space to arguments from both sides (man-made vs natural) although most of the scientific evidence is that we are responsible. They probably do this out of a sense of fairness or just because it provides good viewing, listening or reading. The result is that many people are confused.

Driver

Most people are concerned about their day to day life. Cars are necessary for many people. But they may be persuaded eventually to drive more eco-friendly cars. At the moment, though, such cars are very expensive.

2 Which one of the above do you agree with? Circle your choice and explain why.

Scientist   Environmentalist   Pupil   Driver

Answers will vary.

48   Our warming planet

3 Climate change

This is about how our warming planet may affect us all.

geog.2
pages 94-95

1 Read what is written in the boxes around the map. Draw arrows from each of the boxes to where they may happen on the map. One has been done for you.

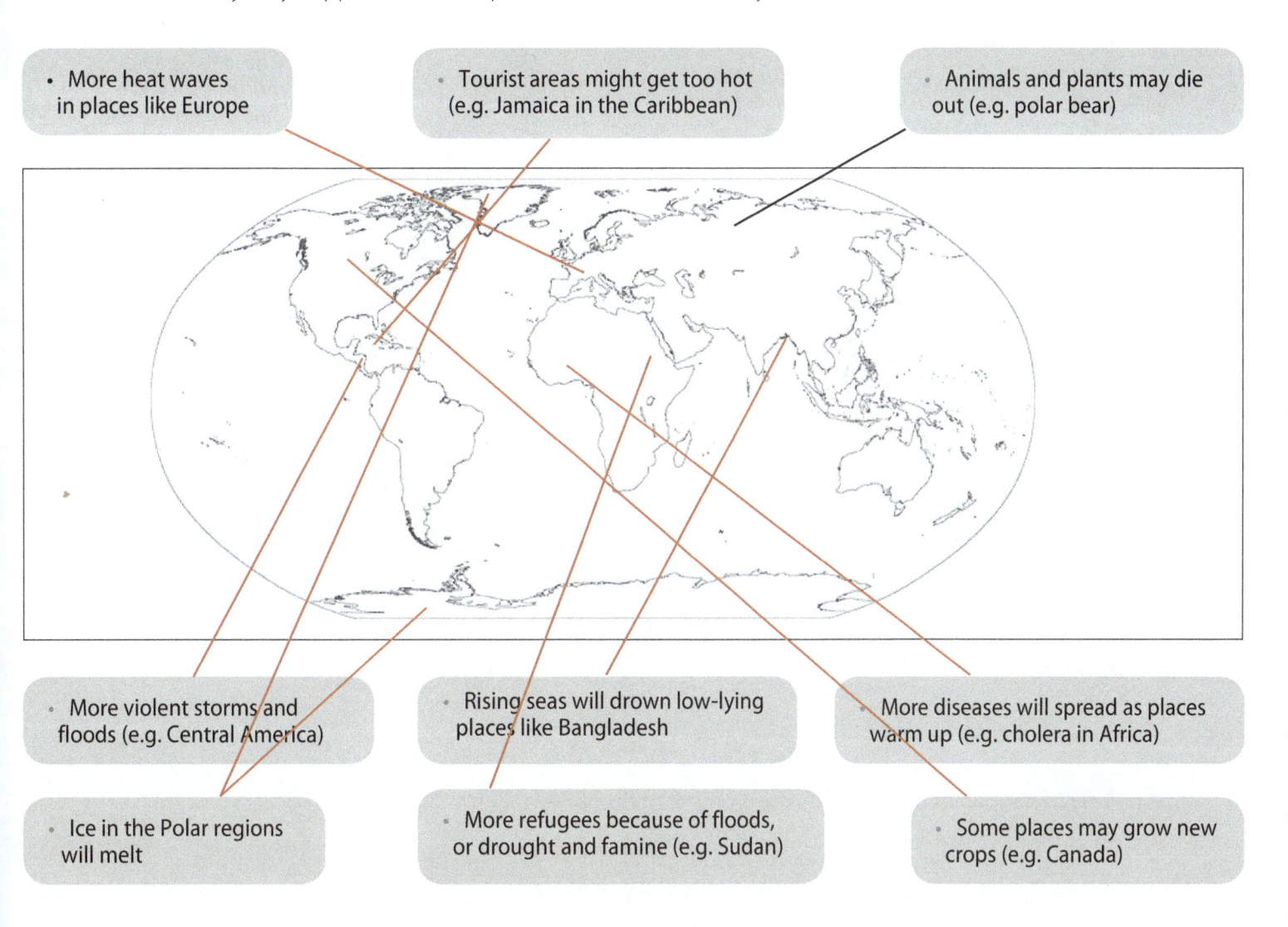

- More heat waves in places like Europe
- Tourist areas might get too hot (e.g. Jamaica in the Caribbean)
- Animals and plants may die out (e.g. polar bear)

- More violent storms and floods (e.g. Central America)
- Rising seas will drown low-lying places like Bangladesh
- More diseases will spread as places warm up (e.g. cholera in Africa)

- Ice in the Polar regions will melt
- More refugees because of floods, or drought and famine (e.g. Sudan)
- Some places may grow new crops (e.g. Canada)

2 Look at the effects of global warming in the boxes. Are any of them good for us?

The only affect in the list above that could be of any benefit would be that of new crops.

Why?

If previously inhospitable areas in the north like Canada and Siberia could grow new crops they could help to feed the growing world population. Eventually they may provide a home for the people displaced by global warming in other areas.

Our warming planet **49**

6.4 It's happening already!

This will make you think about the impact of global warming on human populations

pages 96–97

See the drawings below which tell you about the impact of global warming on two very different animals.

I have to swim further, or starve

I have to spread north – but will I find enough to eat when I get there?

Humans are being affected in the same way.

1. Write about what you think will happen to human populations around the world as global warming increases.

    There will be major movements of people, moving from unproductive and low lying areas. There may be starvation and a high death toll or, to look on the bright side, people may be allowed to colonise hitherto inhospitable areas.

2. What is likely to happen as a result of this movement of humans?

    These movements could lead to potential conflict between nation states. Such refugee crises will hit neighbouring countries to where the crisis has occurred the hardest.

3. Research the impact of global warming on one particular group of people and write about what has happened to them.

    Students could research the inhabitants of Tuvalu and Vanuatu and other Pacific islands who have already had to move because of rising sea levels. Other countries like the Maldives in the Indian Ocean are also feeling the effects.

5 Who will suffer most?

This is about the things we do that produce carbon dioxide.

'Worldmapper' maps are specially drawn maps. They don't show the actual shape and size of each country. They show countries in different sizes depending on what is being measured. Look at the maps below and spot how different the world looks.

This is a map of where toys are from. Toys are made in many parts of the world. Many toys are plastic which is made from oil. The map below shows that China and Hong Kong (on the right) is by far the largest country on the map. This means that it exports, or sells, more toys than any other country.

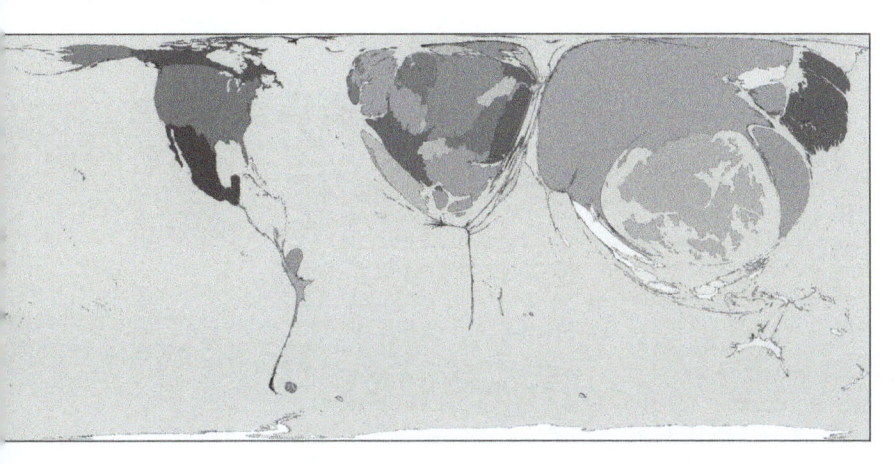

1. Why do you think that China is producing more and more carbon dioxide? Think about the effects of burning oil.

China's drive to improve its standard of living by becoming the new Workshop of the World involves the consumption of huge amounts of energy, including burning fossil fuels. China, to give it credit, is also the world's leading producer of green energy. Everything China does is on a large scale!

The map below shows toy imports (the countries that buy the toys). The USA is now the largest country.

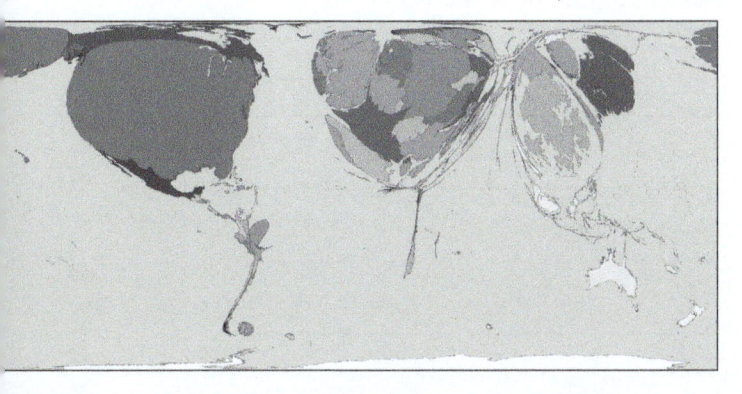

2. This is a very different map. Who should be blamed for increasing oil use – and why?

The US is a major consumer of China's products. Without the demand for these products China would be less polluting.

Our warming planet   51

6.6 So what can we do?

This is about stopping or slowing down global warming.

geog.2
pages 100–101

These actions could help to stop global warming.

Answers will vary. Some of the actions (e.g. relating to energy conservation) are more feasible than others. But students should not be discredited for an imaginative response.

1. Give out free bikes to everyone
2. Breed plants that will gobble up carbon dioxide
3. Put big taxes on air travel
4. Build more windfarms, for electricity
5. Don't turn on the heating. Just put on warm clothes
6. Turn off all the town and city lights at night
7. Shut down all power stations that use oil, coal or gas
8. Allow homes to have electricity for only 6 hours a day
9. Find a way to bury carbon dioxide under the ocean
10. Pass a law that women can only have one child each
11. Shoot millions of small mirrors into space, to reflect some sunlight away
12. Ban international events like the Olympic games

1   Choose **two** of these actions and explain why they may have disadvantages.

Number [ ] _____

_____

Number [ ] _____

_____

2   Choose one of the actions that you think is the best. Write a letter to the Prime Minister explaining your view.

_____
_____
_____
_____
_____
_____

Our warming planet

Asia

geog.2

pages 102-103

1. Test yourself. Without looking anywhere else, draw an outline of Asia in the box below. Then draw in the borders of all the countries you can think of. Include the names of cities, mountains, rivers, lakes and deserts.

> Answers will vary.

2. Write down all you know about three of the places you have put on the map.

   Place 1 _____

   _____

   Place 2 _____

   _____

   Place 3 _____

   _____

3. At the end of this topic, come back and see if you've been correct about these places. Draw a ☺ next to each place you got more or less right. If you were wrong draw a ☹ next to the place!

7.1 What and where is Asia?

This is about locating the continent of Asia on the world map.

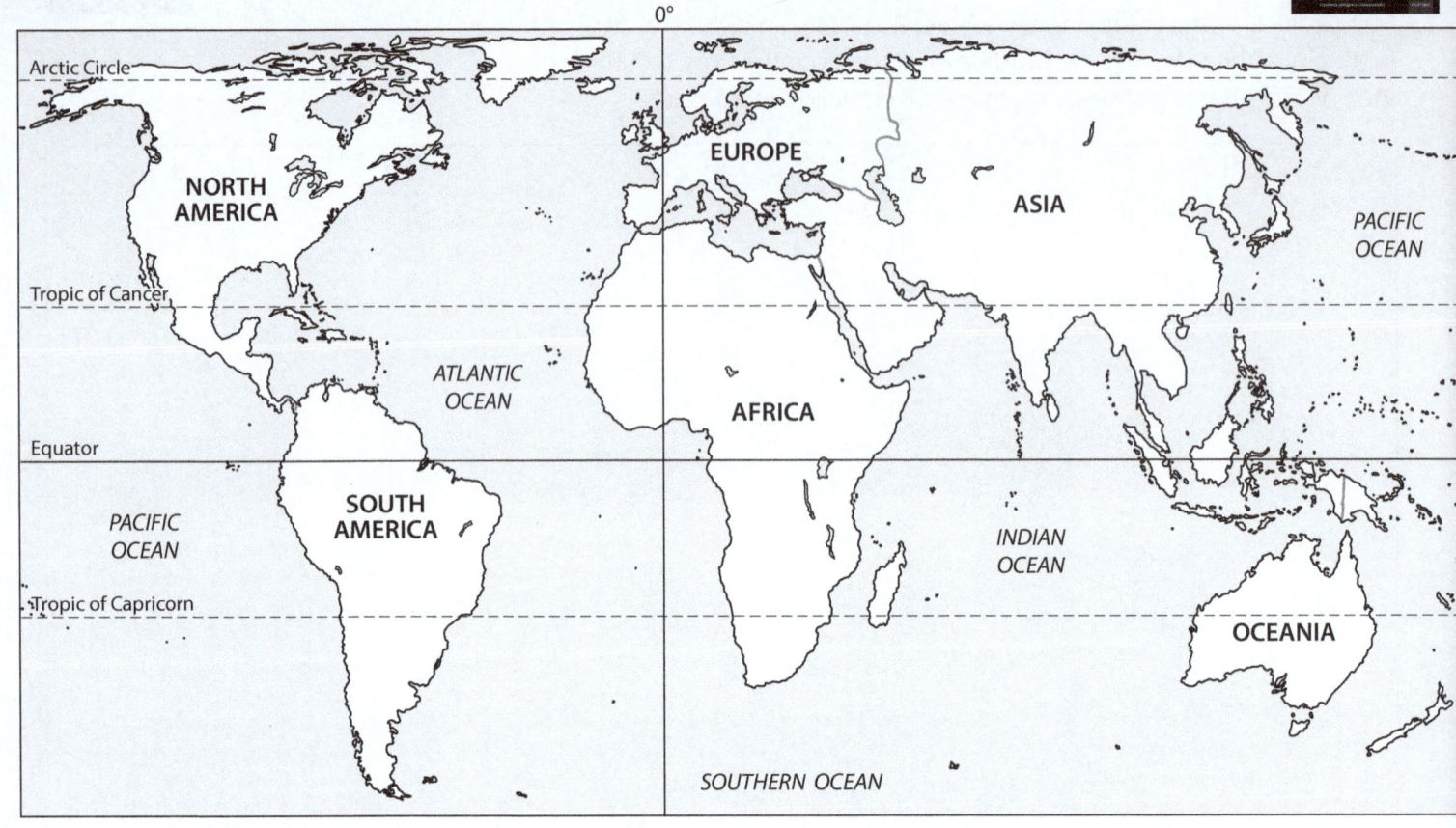

pages 104–105

1. Colour in all the land in Asia that lies between the Tropic of Cancer and the Tropic of Capricorn. This area is known as the 'tropics' and is the hottest part of the world.

2. Using a second colour, colour in all the land in Asia that lies north of the Arctic Circle. This area is known as the Arctic. It is one of the world's two polar regions. They are the coldest parts of the world.

   a Where does Asia have most land – inside the tropics or inside the Arctic Circle?

   Inside the tropics

   b Asia stretches from the tropics to the Arctic. What other continent stretches from the tropics to the Arctic?

   North America

   c Name the island that lies half in Asia, half in Oceania.

   New Guinea

3. Using a third colour fill in all the land area of Asia that lies outside the tropics and outside the Arctic. What proportion of Asia lies neither within the tropics nor within the Arctic? Circle the correct answer.

   A (About 65%)　　　B About 80%　　　C About 50%

4. The map also shows the equator. Shade in the parts of Asia that lie south of the equator.

54　Asia

2 Asia's countries and regions

This will help you understand Asia's size and the variety of its countries and regions.

Write down the names of the capital cities of the following countries

a China __Beijing__ b Iran __Tehran__ c Sri Lanka __Colombo__

d Iraq __Baghdad__ e Cambodia __Phnom Penh__ f Mongolia __Ulan Bator__

g Saudi Arabia __Riyadh__ h Kazakhstan __Alma-ata__ i Pakistan __Islamabad__

Where are the Urals? You can find the Ural Mountains which form the border between Europe and Asia on page 112 of the student book. Draw a line to show them on the map above.

Once you have drawn in the Urals on the map, guess which is the larger, China or Asian Russia?

__Asian Russia__

Find the UK on the map. What is the quickest way to get to the UK by sea from Japan? Why is this not possible for most of the year?

__The quickest way to get from the UK to Japan by sea is by the north-east passage (or Northern sea route), across the north of Russia and through the Bering Straits. It knocks 4000 nautical miles off the journey. Although the ice cover is less now than ever before, it is still only free of ice for around two months of the year.__

Asia 55

7.3 A little history

This will help you understand what we owe to Chinese and Indian civilisations.

1. India is the home of Buddhism. The first emperor to unite India was Ashoka who ruled from 269 to 232 BC. He was converted to Buddhism. Find out more about Ashoka. Why did he convert to Buddhism? Why is he considered to be one of India's greatest rulers?

   Ashoka ruled over most of the Indian sub-continent. After a particularly destructive war he converted to Buddhism. He is remembered as a kind and generous ruler who used Buddhism to unite his people. He left many memorials and inscriptions around India which are a tangible record today of his rule. One famous pillar at Sarnath has become the symbol of modern India.

2. Many important discoveries have been made in China. They include paper (about AD 100), the magnetic compass (about AD 100) and gunpowder (about AD 800).

   Write about how important these discoveries were to us.

   a Paper

   Paper provided a writing surface and later a surface for printing. Before paper arrived European countries had to rely on animal skin (parchment), which was scarce, and papyrus, which was less effective. China was also the first country to introduce paper money.

   b Gunpowder

   Gunpowder was originally discovered accidentally by Chinese alchemists looking for the elixir of immortality. When its destructive force was realised, it was soon put to military purposes. A couple of hundred years later it had spread to Europe (by way of the Mongol conquests) where cannon were developed that changed the shape of warfare.

   c The magnetic compass

   In the 11th century, tiny needles made of magnetized steel were invented in China. One end of the needle points north while the other points south. The compass was thus created. The compass greatly improved a ship's ability to navigate over long distances. It was not until the beginning of the 14th century that the compass was introduced to Europe from China and helped to usher in the great period of European navigation.
   The first person recorded to have used the compass as a navigational aid was Admiral Zheng He, who made seven ocean voyages between 1405 and 1433 which took him to Africa and possibly to the west coast of America.

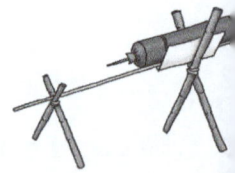

The Chinese used rockets and cannon 600 years before we did.

What's Asia like?

This will help to identify Asia's largest cities and put them into rank order.

Asia, home of the megacity?

Only 42% of the Asia's population lives in urban areas; however, it has the second fastest urban population growth rate, of any continent.
Many claims are made for the growth of Asia's 'megacities'. The figures below for the 20 largest cities in Asia from the United Nations are for the wider built up areas of cities rather than just the actual city boundary.

Place these cities into rank order and identify which country they lie in.

City	Population (millions)	Country	Rank Order
Bangalore	8.45	India	19
Bangkok	8.28	Thailand	20
Beijing	12.39	China	8
Chongqing	9.40	China	14
Delhi	22.16	India	2
Dhaka	14.65	Bangladesh	6
Guangzhou	8.88	China	18
Istanbul	10.52	Turkey	12
Jakarta	9.21	Indonesia	16
Karachi	13.12	Pakistan	7
Kolkata	15.55	India	5
Manila	11.63	Philippines	9
Moscow	10.55	Russia	11
Mumbai	20.04	India	3
Osaka-Kobe	11.34	Japan	10
Seoul	9.77	South Korea	13
Shanghai	16.58	China	4
Shenzhen	9.01	China	17
Tianjin	9.34	China	15
Tokyo	36.67	Japan	1

It is very difficult to find agreement about the size of the world's largest cities. Can you think of reasons why estimates vary?

The population of a city proper has been defined as 'the population living within the administrative boundaries of a city.' But a city as defined by administrative boundaries may not include suburban areas where an important proportion of the population working or studying in the city lives.

Asia

7.5 Asia's physical features

Here we look at the relationship between Asia's physical features and its countries.

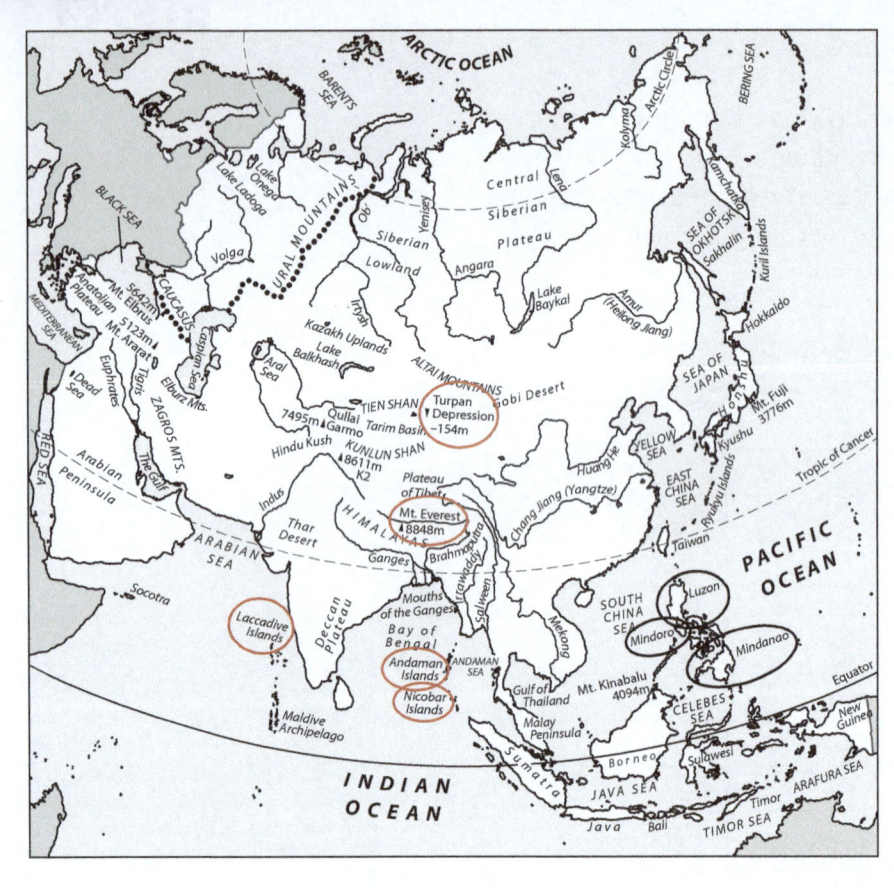

pages 112-113

1. Compare the map on page 112 of the student book with the political map on page 106 and answer the following questions;

    a. Which countries are the Himalayas in?
       India, China, Nepal and Bhutan

    b. In which countries does the Gobi Desert lie
       China and Mongolia

    c. In which country is Lake Baykal?
       Russia

    d. In which country are the Zagros Mountains
       Iran

    e. Name 5 rivers that rise on the Plateau of Tibet
       Choose from: Indus, Mekong, Yangtse, Brahmaputra, Yellow River (Huang He) and Salween

2. On the map:

    a. circle the three groups of islands that are part of India. *Circled in red above.*

    b. circle the highest and lowest points in Asia. What is the difference in height between them? *9002 metres*

    c. Circle the three islands named on the map that are part of the Philippines. *Circled in black above.*

3. Research and find out what is unusual about the Aral Sea.

    Once one of the four largest lakes in the world the Aral Sea has been steadily shrinking since the 1960s after the rivers that fed it were diverted by Soviet irrigation projects. By 2007, it had declined to 10% of its original size. The shrinking of the Aral Sea has been called 'one of the planet's worst environmental disasters'. The region's once-prosperous fishing industry has been destroyed, bringing unemployment and economic hardship. The Aral Sea region is also heavily polluted. The retreat of the sea has reportedly also caused local climate change, with summers becoming hotter and drier, and winters colder and longer.

6 Asia's population

Here we look at the relationship between Asia's population and its physical features.

pages 114–115

Compare the map of Asia's population distribution on page 114 of the student book with the map of Asia's physical features on page 112 of the student book.

In many parts of Asia, but especially in Siberia, the low level density population distribution looks 'stripey'. Can you explain the reason for this?

This is because there is a (relatively) greater population along the banks of Siberia's great rivers.

In the far west of China, near the Mongolian and Kazakhstan borders, there is a city of nearly three million people in an otherwise sparsely populated area. Identify this city and write about its history and its importance today.

Ürümqi, is the capital of Xinjiang Uyghur Autonomous Region of the People's Republic of China, in the northwest of the country. Urumqi was a major hub on the Silk Road during China's Tang dynasty, and developed its reputation as a leading cultural and commercial centre during the Qing dynasty. Ürümqi is situated near the northern route of the Silk Road. Recently, Urumqi has been the scene of violent incidents that Chinese authorities have blamed on radical separatists from the country's Muslim Uighur minority. Tensions between Chinese and ethnic Uighurs in Xinjiang have been simmering for years.

Look up Indonesia on the political and physical maps of Asia on pages 106 and 112 of the student book.

a What do you notice about the population density of Java compared with the other islands of Indonesia?

Java is much more densely populated.

b Can you explain this difference in population density?

Java is a fertile volcanic island; its rice lands are among the richest in the world. It was also the centre of civilisation in the Indonesian archipelago and the home of major Hindu-Buddhist empires before the arrival of Islam. So it was the obvious choice as the centre for the Dutch colonial empire of the East Indies.

The overall population density of Mongolia is 2 people per square kilometre, while the overall population density of China is 139 people per square kilometre. Explain why figures like this can be misleading with reference to the map on page 114 of the student book.

It is clear from the population map on page 114 of the student book that the population of China is very unevenly distributed. At least half of China is as sparsely populated as Mongolia. Students need to be aware that they should look more closely at overall figures like national population densities.

Asia

7.7 Asia's biomes

This is about telling what biome a place is in from its weather statistics.

pages 116-117

The letters on the map represent five cities;

Shanghai   Lhasa   Verkhoyansk   Singapore   Aden

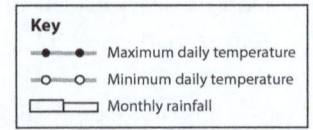

Key
- Maximum daily temperature
- Minimum daily temperature
- Monthly rainfall

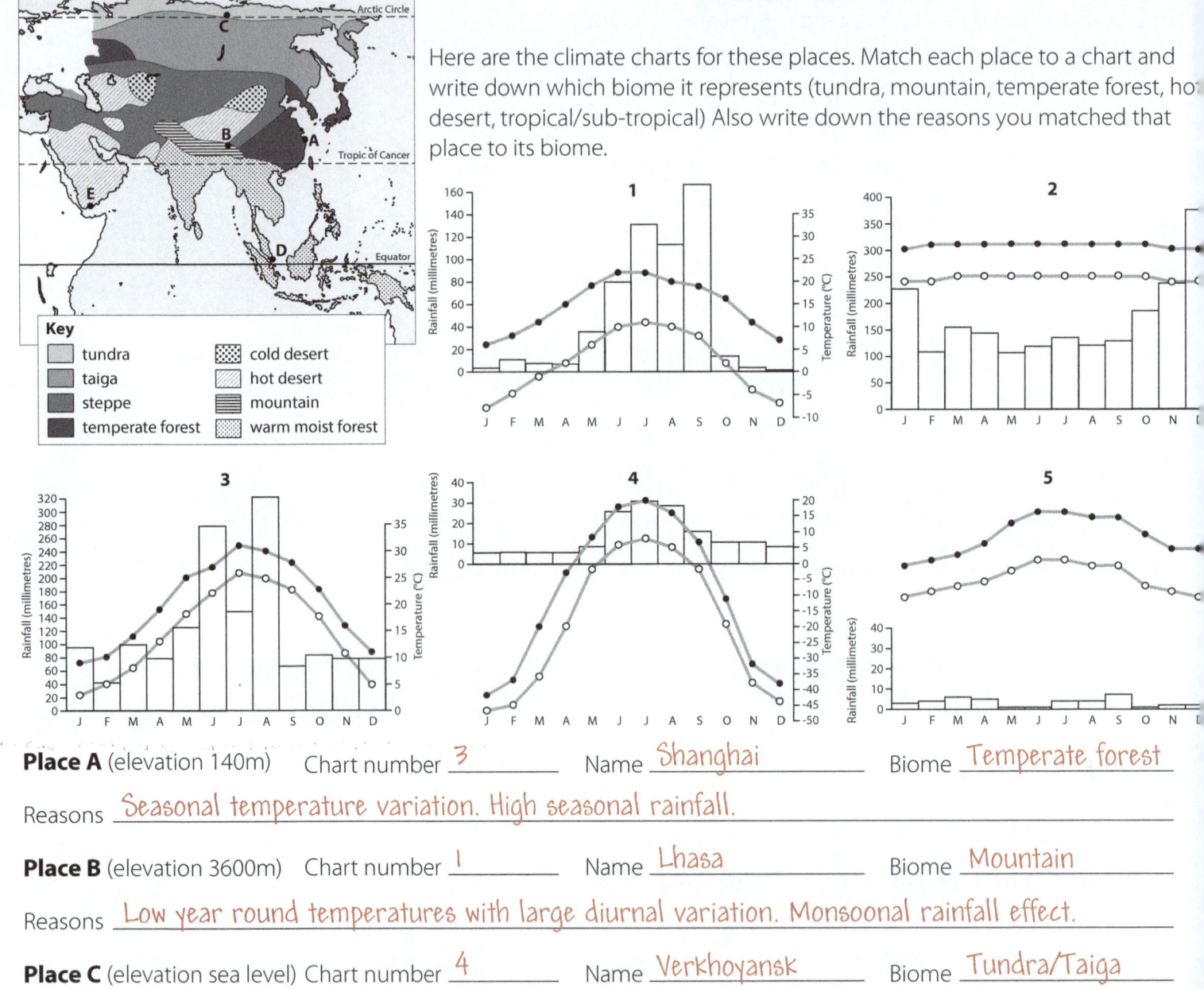

Key (map)
- tundra
- taiga
- steppe
- temperate forest
- cold desert
- hot desert
- mountain
- warm moist forest

Here are the climate charts for these places. Match each place to a chart and write down which biome it represents (tundra, mountain, temperate forest, hot desert, tropical/sub-tropical) Also write down the reasons you matched that place to its biome.

Place A (elevation 140m)   Chart number _3_   Name _Shanghai_   Biome _Temperate forest_

Reasons _Seasonal temperature variation. High seasonal rainfall._

Place B (elevation 3600m)   Chart number _1_   Name _Lhasa_   Biome _Mountain_

Reasons _Low year round temperatures with large diurnal variation. Monsoonal rainfall effect._

Place C (elevation sea level)   Chart number _4_   Name _Verkhoyansk_   Biome _Tundra/Taiga_

Reasons _Severe winter temperatures. Low rainfall._

Place D (elevation sea level)   Chart number _2_   Name _Singapore_   Biome _Warm moist forest_

Reasons _High year round temperatures. High year round rainfall._

Place E (elevation sea level)   Chart number _5_   Name _Aden_   Biome _Hot desert_

Reasons _Extremely high temperatures with large diurnal variation. Very low rainfall._

60   Asia

Southwest China

pages 118-119

Look carefully at the photographs on page 118 in the student book. Imagine you are a web news producer and have been given the images to use in a short video piece for a web site about Southwest China. You have two tasks:

1. Decide in which order you want to present the images. Write the number from 1 to 6 in the tick box top left of each text box.

2. Write a brief commentary to go with each photo. Remember, the website is aiming to introduce Southwest China to people who have not been there!

Pupils should use the photos in a logical sequence and provide a related commentary or sentence to accompany each one.

☐ This photo shows some of the green countryside and landscape of China. Much of the country has rich farmland.

☐ China is not all countryside. It has some of the largest and fastest growing cities on earth.

☐ China is very proud of its culture and heritage and many people still live and dress in a traditional way.

☐ Many Chinese are very religious. Buddhism is the most important religion in the country.

☐ As China grows it has a need for much more energy. One way it can provide this is through using its many rivers to generate hydro-electric power (HEP).

☐ China's industries make many electronic goods, like computers.

8.1 China: an overview

What is blue, a quarter of a mile long and taller than London's Olympic stadium?

1. China is the world's top exporter of goods. Many of the things you buy will have travelled from China on huge container ships like the one described and shown. They can carry 15 000 containers! Find FIVE things that you or your family own that were made in China. Inside the drawing of a container below, sketch and label your five items.

Sketches or drawings of five items made in China, each labelled with its name.

2. Write four sentences to explain why China is so important to your daily life. Remember to include reasons for your answer.

The answer should relate to daily life – home life, shopping, lifestyle – and should have four sentences that may, or may not relate to their answer to Question 1. Example:

China is important to my daily life because many of the things that we use at home are made in China. Without Chinese goods we would not have as many clothes to wear. We might have to buy more expensive clothes made in other countries. We also like Chinese food – it is good to have different types of food to try.

Southwest China

The rise of China

This is about some of the important changes that have happened in China.

geog.2
pages 122-123

Some of the major changes that have affected China are shown below.
Circle whether the statements are true or false.

Changes since 1979	True or False?
Farmers can now farm land for themselves, and sell the extra food they produce	**True** / False
Foreign companies are not allowed to set up in China	True / **False**
All families have to have at least one child	True / **False**
Farmers are allowed to sell the extra food they produce	**True** / False
China trades more with the rest of the world	**True** / False
Forty years ago few Chinese people lived in poverty	True / **False**
The Chinese people were free to make their own choices before the changes	True / **False**

The decisions taken by the Chinese government have led to some successful changes.

- In 1981, 85% of Chinese lived in poverty. Today the figure is about 7%.
- China is now the world's top exporter of manufactured goods.
- China now has the second largest economy in the world, after the USA.
- The one-child policy has prevented around 400 million births.
- Millions of people have moved from rural areas to work in the factories.
- The rate of urbanisation in China is the fastest the world has ever seen.
- China now has many new factories, making goods for export.
- Most new factories are in cities and towns in the east, along and near the coast.

Colour in the one change that you think is most significant to China and its people.
Give reasons for your choice in the space below.

The answer may focus on any of the eight points listed. A good answer will give a reason for choosing the statement, and relate its significance to both the country of China, and its people. For example:

I have chosen 'China is now the world's top exporter of manufactured goods' because trade is how countries can develop and grow. It is important for China because the more money it can earn from foreign trade, the more money it has to spend on developing its country even more (e.g. building roads and hospitals). It is good for the people because they can get jobs in the factories that make the goods, and they will also benefit from the new roads and hospitals.

Southwest China   63

8.3 China's Southwest region

This is where you will learn more about the Southwest region of China.

geog.2
pages 124–125

	Population (millions)	Population density (people per km²)	% of population that is urban	GDP per person PPP (dollars)
Tibet	3	2.2	15	6138
Sichuan	81	170	33	7642
Chongqing	30	350	49	10 077
Guizhou	35	200	35	3100
Yunnan	46	120	33	4160
UK	64	263	80	37 000

1   Study the data about Southwest China.

   a   How many times larger is the population of Chongqing than Tibet? __10 times larger__

   b   In which area do almost half the people live in towns and cities? __Chongqing__

   c   Which part of Southwest China has a GDP that is $4 542 less than Sichuan? __Guizhou__

   d   What percentage of Tibet's population lives in the countryside? __85%__

2   On the map label the five smaller areas of Southwest China – Tibet, Sichuan, Chongqing, Guizhou and Yunnan.

3   In the table below, choose and write down three interesting facts about each of the five areas.

Answers may be taken from any aspect of pages 124–5. Answers such as those shown below would be acceptable.

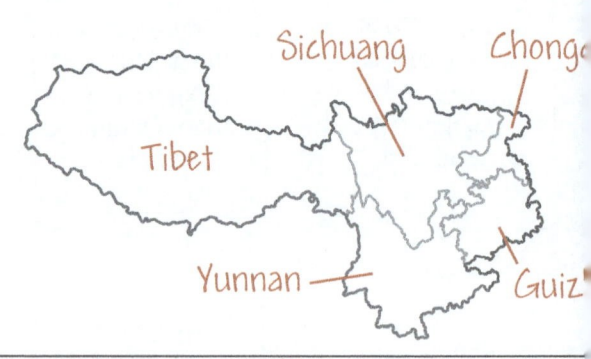

Map labels: Sichuang, Chongq, Tibet, Yunnan, Guiz

Tibet	• Smallest and quietest area of Southwest China • Most mountainous • Coldest • Many rivers flow through • Most people live in the countryside • The poorest area of Southwest China
Sichuan	• Contrasting scenery – some mountains some farming • Important farming and wine-producing region • Many hi-tech factories
Chongqing	• Based on an inland port not on the coast • A fast growing area • Most densely populated area of the region • The richest part of Southwest China
Guizhou	• A farming area • Tobacco and rubber are the main crops • Large (40%) ethnic population leads to rich culture
Yunnan	• Tobacco and coffee growing areas • Mild climate • Interesting Karst scenery • Not a crowded part of Southwest China

4   Choose the one area which you would like to visit most, and give reasons for your answer.

   I would most like to visit …

Answers relating to personal preferences, such as quiet/busy, scenery, possible activities (e.g. mountain climbing), accessibility, cultural similarities/differences, wealth/poverty.

64   Southwest China

Chongqing

Hold onto your seats – this area is growing fast!

Fill in the gaps in the following passage using words from the box below.

Chongqing is controlled from __Beijing__. It is a little __bigger__ than Scotland and most of it is __rural__. Chongqing city lies at the confluence of two rivers; this means where the rivers __meet__. Chongqing is an inland port. This means that large __ships__ can travel from the port of __Shanghai__, 2380 km away. There are many __manufacturing__ industries, making products such as cars, textiles and computers. Farmers in the rural areas keep pigs, and grow rice and __oranges__.

| bigger | rural | ships | oranges |
| meet | Shanghai | manufacturing | Beijing |

Chongqing city is growing fast and many people are moving there. In the speech bubbles below write what these people would think about the developments in the city. Remember to give reasons for your answers!

The pupils should decide and state whether the developments are good/positive or bad/negative. Answers should also relate both to the reason for moving to Chongqing and their perceptions of the benefits of what it will be like there. Positive aspects that may be mentioned are job opportunities, newly-built environment to live and work, the chance to be part of a vibrant and growing city and a ready and increasing pool of employees from which to choose.
Some negative views may revolve around the noise from the building work, the range of potential dangers from living and working in a large city (traffic, crime, etc.) and possibly sense of isolation if moving from the countryside.

My company is just setting up an office here. I think the developments in the city are …

I've moved here for a new job. I think the developments in the city are …

I want to start a new business in Chongqing. The government …

Southwest China 65

8.5 Life in Chongqing

This is about the lives of some of the people who live and work in Chongqing.

> Pupils should circle a number that represents the happiness of each of the four people. They should then go on to justify why they have chosen that number. The best answers may relate the happiness score they have chosen to the HPI categories: life expectancy, life well-being and ecological footprint. Suggested answers for each person are given below.

1 China has a Happy Planet Index of 44.7 and is ranked at number 60 out of 151 countries. How happy do you think Liu Jian, Wang Hua, Wu Shan and He Chan feel? Circle the number for each of them on the scale below and give reasons to explain your choice.

Happiness Scale

Liu Jian, a bang-bang man

Very Unhappy 0 — 1 — 2 — 3 — 4 — 5 Very Happy

Reason for decision

Unhappy – still poor, no skills, work is hard, he is living (7 hours) away from his family.
Happy – lives in shared accommodation for a reasonable rent, able to send home money to family.

Wang Hua, factory worker

Very Unhappy 0 — 1 — 2 — 3 — 4 — 5 Very Happy

Reason for decision Unhappy – living apart from son (150km away), does not have full city rights, feels like a second-class citizen. Happy – better pay than previous job in noodle bar, lives in a flat with friends, opportunity for urban hukou.

Wu Shan, restaurant owner

Very Unhappy 0 — 1 — 2 — 3 — 4 — 5 Very Happy

Reason for decision

Unhappy – village of birth drowned when Three Gorges Dam was built.
Happy – owns two restaurants, likes the lively city, loves cooking and is making money.

He Chan, a left behind

Very Unhappy 0 — 1 — 2 — 3 — 4 — 5 Very Happy

Reason for decision Unhappy – lives apart from parents, would like to move to city to be with rest of family.
Happy – lives with gran, parents bring presents when they visit, loves Chinese New Year, often talks to parents on phone, good schooling.

Southwest China

Tops for biodiversity!

Panda-monium - this is all about China's panda population.

pages 130-131

1 Read these statements about China's and its pandas.

A "Sichuan's panda sanctuaries are home to around a third of the world's population of pandas."

B "Seven nature reserves and nine parks lie next to the Qionglai and Jiajin mountains. The sanctuaries are also home to red pandas, snow and cloud leopards."

C "Pandas are the poster animals for the zoo industry. They receive millions of pounds worth of support. I think this money would be better spent preserving their habitat instead so that they can stay in the wild."

D "Bamboo is the main food of pandas. It is estimated that half of the world bamboo forests have disappeared since 1974."

E "In May 2013 the world's first panda-themed hotel opened for business in Sichuan."

F "Most captive-breeding programs eventually want to reintroduce the animals back into China's bamboo forests – but can they survive in the forests?"

G "In Ya'an, about an hour and a half away from the city of Chengdu, tourism chiefs aim to create a giant panda capital."

H "Possibly as few as 1,600 giant pandas remain in the wild, and more than 300 live in captivity around the globe"

Using the information above, write a 70 word speech explaining your view about pandas and their survival.

Tip: Be as persuasive as you can!

The speech (around 70 words) should use the information given above, be persuasive and should offer a point of view. An example might be:
Pandas are an endangered species as there are only around 1600 left in the world. More than 300 live in captivity, many of them in China. I think that more should be done to protect the pandas but letting them back into the wild might mean that numbers go down as the bamboo forests which they live in are being cut down for farming. I think we should look after them because we should not let a species die.

Suggest one idea that you think will have most chance of helping pandas to survive. Give reasons for your answer.

An example might be:
I think that we need to educate people more about the dangers of cutting down bamboo forests. If people are educated they will understand the problem better and may give money to help the scientists look after the pandas. This would then mean that more pandas survive.

Southwest China 67

8.7 Tibet

Here you will find out more about Tibet, China's 'Roof of the World'.

pages 132-133

1. This paragraph describes Tibet. Choose words from the box to fill in the gaps.

   Tibet is over ten times _____ than the UK and over 4.5 km _high_ on average. At the _southern_ edge of the plateau, the Himalayas begin. Tibet is cold, and the winds can be _vicious_. Much of the country is Tundra, with permanently frozen soil and no _trees_. Tibet is _dry_ for nine months of the year, but has thousands of _____ and lakes.

   | high dry trees vicious wet glaciers southern people bigger reservoirs |

2. Explain why Tibet is often called the 'Roof of the World'.

   Tibet is called the 'Roof on the World' because it has an average height of over 4.5km above sea level, and is close to the two highest mountains on Earth, Mount Everest and K2. It is one of the highest regions on the planet.

3. An extreme environment has harsh and challenging conditions – because of its location, its ecosystem, climate or landscape. Humans and animals often need to adapt in order to survive in it. To what extent do you think Tibet is an extreme environment? Give reasons for your answer.

   Tip: Use facts and figures from the student book pages to help you decide!

   In a good answer the student would say whether they thought Tibet was an extreme environment or not. It should refer to Tibet's location, its ecosystem, climate and landscape. It would also refer to at least one adaption made by people or animals in order to live there.
   Example:
   I think Tibet is a very extreme environment. It is one of the highest regions on Earth, nearly 4.5 km above sea level on average and in a very remote area of Asia. Much of the ground is frozen which means that it is very difficult for plants and animals to survive there. People and animals need to have, or grow, thick coats if they are able to survive!

4. 'Earth bit hiss' is an anagram for three words that could be used to describe Tibet.
   Can you decode the anagram? _Tibet is harsh_

   Do you agree? Give reasons for your answer.

   An example might be:
   I do agree because it is very difficult for people to live and work there because it is so cold and very remote from other people and places.

Southwest China

All change in Tibet

This is about some of the important changes happening in Tibet.

1 Using your own words annotate the photograph below to explain why China is making some of the changes in Tibet.

> Tip: Think of the reasons, and what benefits the changes may bring to Tibet.

Transport

So that people and goods can be moved more easily between different areas of the country. This will allow more parts of the country to develop its industry, which will help the economy to grow.

Mining

So that the oil, gas and metal industries can grow. This will help create jobs and wealth and help to provide China's raw materials for its growing population.

Water

A growing population and industrial development both require increased quantities of water.

Land

As China's population grows it needs more land for both settlements and for industry. As much of Tibet is mountainous, it needs to use what land it can to allow its developments.

Imagine you are one of the local people shown in the photograph. What would you think about the changes? Choose the one that you think would benefit you the most. Explain your answer.

Answers should give a view about the changes planned, and then choose one of the changes and explain why that change would be of most benefit.

I think that the changes in Tibet will

help the country become more developed and bring jobs and wealth to the region. It will also make it easier for us to travel to other areas of Tibet and China. However, many of the changes may have a bad effect on the environment and the natural beauty of the area. This may put tourists off visiting.

The one change that would most benefit me is

Transport: easier access to, and from, other parts of the country, both for industries and for individual people. This may improve employment chances for people in this region.
Mining: All industry needs raw materials. If industry develops, then we all have a chance of gaining jobs which will give us money to help improve our lives.
Water: We all need water. As the population of the country grows so does the demand for water, for drinking, washing and for all types of industrial use.
Land: If settlements are built we may have access to more services like schools and hospitals.

8.9 The rivers and dams

This is all about China's big plans for building dams.

geog.2
pages 136-137

1 This wordsearch is all about China and its plans to capture its water. Find the words shown on the right.

```
m m j p w u f e z r b z w p g
s e w j a r l l o t q r t l r
r f l y r e v e y s m s o q q
e m q t m s u c a m t b h c b
i i v o i g z t e a a y j a e
c n v w n n n r t l m m l a n
a f w l g j g i n c j b r a s
l a p o l w b c q s c t j c e
g h r h r a t i c g h c n q e
a z h p h d t t h q n h b j r
p l a t e a u y u r m o p m t
p f y a d g h a z o l p h t p
n g g q z i k y k n j e u c i
e z u d j e n o i t u l l o p
w b z j s r e t a w x g n m h
```

chongqing(14,13,NW)
drown(6,10,NW)
earthquakes(15,5,SW)
electricity(8,1,S)
glaciers(1,9,N)
global(15,1,SW)
habitats(5,10,NE)
melting (1,1,SE)
plateau(1,11,E)
pollution(15,14,W)
trees(15,11,N)
warming(5,1,S)
water(10,15,W)

2 In the space below, write a paragraph about China and its dams. You must use all of the words that you found in the wordsearch!

The best answers will be made up of logical sentences that use each of the words from the wordsearch. An example might be:

As **Chongqing** city grows there is a need for more **water**. China has many rivers flowing off the **Plateau** of Tibet, which get their water from **melting glaciers**. Much of the water may be used to make **electricity**, because burning coal in power stations is a big source of **pollution**. However, there are problems. The lakes formed by dams **drown** the land, **trees** are chopped down and **habitats** destroyed. Dams may be at risk from **earthquakes** and, because of **global warming**, the glaciers may melt which means the rivers have less water.

70 Southwest China

geog.2 workbook answer book

4th edition

This answer book gives you vital support for the geog.2 workbook. Each page matches the workbook and the answers are written in colour, so they're easy and quick to use for marking or reference. geog.123 is a three-book course for the National Curriculum at Key Stage 3.

Did you know?
- So far, the highest wave ever surfed was 24.3 m ...
- ... off the coast of Portugal.

What if...
- ... aliens abducted all the children?

Did you know?
- Deserts are places with less than 25 cm of rain a year.
- Some deserts are hot, some cold.

kerboodle

Kerboodle provides digital Lessons, Resources and Assessment for your classroom, plus a Kerboodle Online Student Book available for separate access by teachers and students.

Also available
geog.2 workbook   ISBN 978 0 19 839306 1
geog.2 workbook – pack of 10   ISBN 978 0 19 839300 9

Printed on paper produced from sustainable forests.

OXFORD
UNIVERSITY PRESS

How to get in touch:
web   www.oxfordsecondary.co.uk
email schools.enquiries.uk@oup.com
tel   +44 (0)1536 452620
fax   +44 (0)1865 313472

ISBN 978-0-19-835692-9